Cheatham County, Tennessee

Marriages

1856 – 1881

Byron and Barbara Sistler

JANAWAY PUBLISHING, INC.
Santa Maria, California

Originally Published:
Nashville, Tennessee
1988

Reprinted by

Janaway Publishing, Inc.
732 Kelsey Ct.
Santa Maria, California 93454
(805) 925-1038
www.JanawayGenealogy.com

2006, 2013

ISBN: 978-1-59641-052-7

Made in the United States of America

CHEATHAM COUNTY, TN MARRIAGES
1856-1881

Where two dates appear on an entry, the first one is the date license was issued, the second (in parentheses) the date marriage was solemnized. If only one date, it usually means that the date of execution was the same as the date of license issuance.

Sometimes the execution of the marriage was not reported to the courthouse, and occasionally the clerk failed to note in the marriage book that the license was returned. We would usually make a notation in the entry to indicate the non-execution of a marriage if the book so stated.

The marriages are arranged alphabetically, the first half of the book by groom--the second by bride.

The records included in this book were transcribed by us directly from microfilmm of the original marriage books. Error, where it occurs, may be attributed to us, or to the clerks of the period, many of whom did an appallingly sloppy job of entering the information.

If the bride and groom were black, a B is placed at the end of the entry.

It should be remembered that this and other marriage books we have prepared are indexes, and do not include all the information to be found in the original marriage book. Such data as names of bondsmen, ministers, justices of the peace, churches, etc., are omitted. Often such information is helpful to the researcher. Consequently the serious researcher, to obtain this additional information as well as to check on the accuracy of the transcriber, should examine the original marriage record if at all possible.

Byron Sistler
Barbara Sistler

Nashville, TN
January 1988

Abanathy, Laban to Mary Carney 2-27-1865   [Ce]
Abanathy, S. T. to M. A. T. Demumbra 7-14-1857   [Ce]
Abanathy, S. Y. to M. A. T. Demumbra 7-14-1857 (7-17-1857) [Ce]
Abshere, Calvin to Buthinda M. J. Liles 7-11-1868 (7-22-1868) [Ce]
Adams, Henry to Lucinda McCay 9-1-1864   [Ce]
Adams, J. W. to V. C. Work 9-25-1880 (9-26-1880) [Ce]
Adcock, Clay to Sallie Doolin 3-19-1877   [Ce]
Adcock, Franklin to Nancy Jane Wilson 8-25-1866 (8-30-1866)   [Ce]
Adkins, H.U. to Mary J. McCormack 2-5-1867 (2-6-1867) [Ce]
Adkisson, George to Lilly Bell 12-24-1878 B [Ce]
Adkisson, Phillip to Julia Cooper 9-16-1867 (9-23-1867) B [Ce]
Adkisson, T. J. to A. T. Hale 1-10-1866   [Ce]
Adkisson, W. T. to M.J. Hampton 2-19-1861 (2-20-1861) [Ce]
Aken, A. B. to Judith A. Dunn 1-13-1864   [Ce]
Aker?, Jessee to Josephine Hudgens 12-22-1879 B [Ce]
Albritton, Frank to Ellen Lee Hudgens 3-24-1880   [Ce]
Allen, A. F. to J. S. Hale 5-11-1872 (5-12-1872) [Ce]
Allen, C. F. to Martha A. Ford 7-11-1870   [Ce]
Allen, Geo. M. to Harrett A. Knight 7-3-1880   [Ce]
Allen, Green to Mary A. Green 12-14-1860   [Ce]
Allen, J. B. to J. J. Hollis 1-17-1878 (no return) [Ce]
Allen, J. R. to Susan J. Morris 9-14-1880 (9-16-1880) [Ce]
Allen, John N. to Lucada F. Jordan 4-15-1876 (4-16-1876)   [Ce]
Allen, Lewis to Perlina Overton 9-16-1869 B [Ce]
Alley, Isaac W. to Mary Bracy 12-25-1857   [Ce]
Alley, James to F. Morton 1-11-1857 (1-15-1857) [Ce]
Alley, S. B. to Josephine Hooper 5-1-1869 (5-2-1869) [Ce]
Alwell, George to Ann E. Williams 6-21-1869 (7-1-1869) [Ce]
Anderson, Augustin to Charlotte V. Gatewood 8-15-1880   [Ce]
Anderson, C. W. to Mary A. Bone 3-7-1861   [Ce]
Anderson, Charles E. to Martha A. Alley 9-16-1874 (9-20-1874) [Ce]
Anderson, Frank A. to Lu Bonnett 8-22-1871   [Ce]
Anderson, George to Elizabeth Felts 10-10-1866 (10-11-1866)   [Ce]
Anderson, James H. to Susan Turner 12-24-1859   [Ce]
Andrews, Peter to Nancy Benningfield 4-19-1875   [Ce]
Andrews, Peter to Sarah A. Stinnett 3-6-1877 (3-7-1877) [Ce]
Anglin, Jeff to Emma Binkley 5-25-1881 B [Ce]
Appleton, C. H. to P. I. Clark 6-11-1860 (6-14-1860) [Ce]
Appleton, John to Maggie Russell 6-23-1875   [Ce]
Arcly?, Andrew to Dicy Jane Knight 11-18-1868 (11-19-1868) [Ce]
Armstead, Anthony to Rose Shelton 12-15-1877 (12-16-1877) B [Ce]
Arrington, J. D. to Jennie L. Sanders 8-25-1869   [Ce]
Askins, W. M. to M. T. Sisler? 2-10-1872 (2-11-1872) [Ce]
Babb, J. M. to George A. Binkley 8-17-1874 (8-19-1874) [Ce]
Baggett, H. W. to Virginia Stack 10-26-1878 (10-31-1878) [Ce]
Baggett, R. B. to Samantha Swift 10-13-1879 (10-15-1879) [Ce]
Bagwell, John M. to Caroline Mays 9-7-1859 (9-8-1859) [Ce]
Bailey, W. T. to E. B. Nicholson 12-27-1873 (12-28-1873) [Ce]
Baker, Hiram B. to Sarah M. F. Higgins 8-26-1867 (8-29-1867)   [Ce]
Baker, W. C. to V. H. Whitfield 12-24-1877 (12-25-1877) [Ce]
Balden, Alick to Barber A. Walker 4-23-1870 (5-1-1870) [Ce]
Balthrop, Peter to Berty Nichols 11-27-1874 (11-28-1874) B [Ce]
Balthrop, Samuel to Harriet Hudgens 9-21-1872 (9-22-1872) B [Ce]

Balthrop, Thos. T. to Mary E. Hunter 12-11-1868 (12-15-1868) [Ce]
Balum, G. W. to Mary E. Andrews 2-20-1879 (2-23-1879) B [Ce]
Barclift, Thos. C. to Charlotte Smith 1-4-1858 (1-5-1858) [Ce]
Barnes, B. J. to G. A. Stewart 1-3-1859 (1-4-1859) [Ce]
Barnes, B. J. to Julia A. Binkley 11-18-1858 [Ce]
Barnes, J. T. to Rosetta Cagle 5-25-1876 [Ce]
Bartee, J. B. to A. T. Woodward 12-6-1859 (12-13-1859) [Ce]
Barton, Alex to Edna Williams 1-29-1880 B [Ce]
Barton, Charles to Harriet Majors 12-27-1870 (12-31-1870) B [Ce]
Barton, Granville to Edna Willis 3-17-1877 (3-18-1877) B [Ce]
Barton, Robert to Sarah Chambliss 1-27-1873 (1-30-1873) B [Ce]
Basford, G. W. to Mary Frey 9-6-1875 (9-8-1875) [Ce]
Basford, Geo. W. to Elizabeth Miles 11-15-1858 (11-17-1858) [Ce]
Basford, J. J. to Eller Trainum 10-4-1869 (10-14-1869) [Ce]
Basford, James to Louisa Pascal 7-5-1877 (7-31-1877) [Ce]
Basford, John to Nancy J. Jackson 11-22-1866 [Ce]
Bass, Evans to Mary Frazier 1-11-1871 B [Ce]
Batson, J. H. to S. L. Hagwood 9-10-1879 (9-11-1879) [Ce]
Batson, John to Fanny Head 1-28-1871 B [Ce]
Batts, J. H. to M. E. Hunter 12-16-1879 [Ce]
Batts, John to Y.? W. Pool 12-23-1857 [Ce]
Baxter, John to Josephine Knight 8-3-1874 [Ce]
Bean, Alexander to Mary Neighbors 11-1-1875 (11-3-1875) [Ce]
Bearden, Augustus to Martha Coleman 6-2-1858 (6-3-1858) [Ce]
Beck, David to Martha Holt 4-14-1871 B [Ce]
Becker?, S. H. to M. S. Frazier 3-6-1875 (3-7-1875) [Ce]
Beele, George W. to Everline Krantz 8-18-1879 [Ce]
Bell, J. B. to M. M. Pack 1-17-1876 (1-19-1876) [Ce]
Bell, J. P. to M. P. Carter 9-26-1879 [Ce]
Bell, John to Mary A. Harris 12-22-1866 (12-25-1866) B [Ce]
Bell, John to Minty Lee 6-11-1856 [Ce]
Bell, Thos. to Nancy A. Williams 10-10-1871 (10-11-1871) [Ce]
Bell, Thos. F. to Mary Binkley 11-5-1863 [Ce]
Bell, W. T. to Amanda E. Walker 2-13-1873 [Ce]
Bell, Willy to Louisa Woodmore 9-27-1876 (9-28-1876) B [Ce]
Bennett, J. J. to Susan E. Ventress 11-26-1879 [Ce]
Bennett, Jacob to Elizabeth Mosier 7-8-1865 [Ce]
Bennett, Jacob to Tabitha Morris 1-17-1857 (1-18-1857) [Ce]
Bennett, Jessee to W. A. Mosier 2-10-1866 [Ce]
Bennett, John to Josephine Farmer 2-22-1877 (2-23-1877) [Ce]
Benningfield, Y. W. to Elizabeth Smith 2-21-1868 (2-25-1868) [Ce]
Bess, John to Eliz. Rose 12-2-1857 [Ce]
Bethune, R. M. to Sarah A Stack 1-1-1868 (1-2-1868) [Ce]
Biggar, Thomopson to Mary Ella Bright 1-6-1879 (1-8-1879) [Ce]
Biggin, J. H. to S. A. Hooper 11-22-1856 [Ce]
Biggs, Charlie T. to Catie Barnes 4-28-1879 [Ce]
Biggs, W. A. to Susana Vick 1-15-1872 (1-14?-1872) [Ce]
Binkley, A. F. to Mary Isabelle Boyd 12-20-1873 (12-26-1873) [Ce]
Binkley, A. J. to Kissie Harris 2-28-1865 [Ce]
Binkley, A. M. to Charlotte F. Morris 10-2-1869 (10-3-1869) [Ce]
Binkley, Adam to Izora? Stewart 11-14-1866 (11-15-1866) [Ce]
Binkley, B. B. to Sallie McCormick 7-27-1864 (7-28-1864) [Ce]
Binkley, Buck to Hannah Watson 2-2-1870 (2-6-1870) B [Ce]
Binkley, F. P. to Mary M. S. Krantz 9-14-1874 (9-20-1874) [Ce]

Binkley, G. W. to Emily M. Gibbs 6-14-1862   [Ce]
Binkley, G. W. to M. A. Rose 7-20-1859 (7-21-1859)   [Ce]
Binkley, Geo. W. to Martha F. Felts 6-29-1864   [Ce]
Binkley, George to Lucind Binkley 8-18-1871 B [Ce]
Binkley, George F. to Martha V. Smith 11-17-1873 (12-19-1873)   [Ce]
Binkley, H. J. to Margret L. Hunt 4-17-1858   [Ce]
Binkley, H. J. to Susan R. Sanders 8-3-1872 (8-4-1872)   [Ce]
Binkley, H. W. to Elizabeth Morris 9-23-1867 (9-2?-1867)   [Ce]
Binkley, Henry to Mary Morris 2-5-1876 (2-6-1876)   [Ce]
Binkley, James to Nancy E. Read 9-3-1859 (9-4-1859)   [Ce]
Binkley, James M. to Catharine Arington 6-29-1864   [Ce]
Binkley, James S. to Mandelia Cagle 12-14-1872 (12-19-1872)   [Ce]
Binkley, Jo to Nancy Demumbra 1-8-1862   [Ce]
Binkley, John R. to Eliza Morris 5-19-1866 (5-20-1866)   [Ce]
Binkley, John R. to Katharine Binkley 12-10-1857   [Ce]
Binkley, Lenard to Sarah Foster 3-25-1864   [Ce]
Binkley, Lenard to Tabitha Carney 12-16-1858   [Ce]
Binkley, Leonard to M. J. Williams 12-3-1864   [Ce]
Binkley, Leonard to Tabitha Bennett 8-16-1862   [Ce]
Binkley, Levingston to Roxzaner Smith 6-12-1869   [Ce]
Binkley, M. to Nancy Felts 10-15-1866 (10-17-1866)   [Ce]
Binkley, Monroe to Martha Binkley 8-2-1866   [Ce]
Binkley, Montgomery to Mary Bennett 1-23-1858 (1-24-1858)   [Ce]
Binkley, N. N. to N. A. R. F. Read 12-12-1857   [Ce]
Binkley, T. M. to Martha Newman 8-5-1876 (8-7-1876)   [Ce]
Binkley, Thos. J. to Cytha P. Goddard 12-23-1868   [Ce]
Black, John C. to H. A. Dismukes 1-16-1861 (1-17-1861)   [Ce]
Blankenship, A. S. to Sarah T. Gupton 11-21-1868 (11-22-1868)   [Ce]
Blankinship, W. b. to Susan Gibbs 3-5-1878 (3-6-1878)   [Ce]
Bobbett, Stephen to Virginia Bobbett 12-6-1859   [Ce]
Bobbett, Wm. J. to Nancy Miles 1-2-1867 (1-3-1867)   [Ce]
Bobbitt, J. D. to Sarah E. Stewart 11-25-1870 (11-27-1870)   [Ce]
Bobbitt, L. S.? to Nancy J. Simmons 1-27-1876 (1-30-1876)   [Ce]
Bobett, J. P. to Elizabeth Watt 10-1-1866 (10-3-1866)   [Ce]
Boling, John H. to Martha Jane Tettar? 7-6-1872 (7-7-1872)   [Ce]
Bone, William W. to Nancy Ramer 10-15-1864   [Ce]
Boyd, G. W. to Sarah C. Demumbra 6-26-1862   [Ce]
Boyd, Geo. W. to Nancy J. Carney 6-28-1876 (6-29-1876)   [Ce]
Boyd, Jessee to Rebecca F. Demumbra 12-23-1869 (12-24-1869)   [Ce]
Boyd, John to Harriet D. Binkley 10-19-1867   [Ce]
Boyd, Thomas to Nancy Sherron 4-7-1873 (4-9-1873)   [Ce]
Boyd, William to Martha Birthright 12-19-1877 (12-27-1877)   [Ce]
Boyd, Wilson to Louisa Buckley 1-14-1878   [Ce]
Boyle, James H. to Judith Pattin 7-15-1880   [Ce]
Boyt, David A. to Malvina McCormack 12-7-1876 (12-8-1876)   [Ce]
Boyt, F. G. to Lucy A. Binkley 2-13-1861   [Ce]
Boyte, Alex. E. to Susan M. Henderson 4-5-1879 (4-6-1879)   [Ce]
Boyte, Felix G. to Parlee Binkley 3-9-1868 (6-14-1868)   [Ce]
Boyte, G. W. to Nannie Obrien 3-16-1878   [Ce]
Boyte, W. J. to A. T. Sanders 6-29-1872 (6-30-1872)   [Ce]
Bradley, James E. to Fredonia A. Hooper 2-7-1861   [Ce]
Bradley, T. P. to Mary E. Sanders 2-17-1869 (2-18-1869)   [Ce]
Bradley, W. L. to J. T. Hudgens 7-5-1858 (7-8-1858)   [Ce]
Bratton, William to Laura Anderson 12-10-1863   [Ce]

3

Brian, R. W. to E. A. Inman 9-10-1867 (9-12-1867) [Ce]
Bright, B. B. to Rebecca Stewart 7-15-1857 (8-3-1857) [Ce]
Bright, James L. to Martha Holmes 2-20-1862 [Ce]
Bright, James W. to Sarah M. Pool 11-29-1873 (11-30-1873) [Ce]
Bright, W. L. to E. Adcock 7-8-1865 (7-16-1865) [Ce]
Bright, William to Elizabeth Holmes 9-6-1861 [Ce]
Bright, Wm. T. to Nelia Boyd 10-21-1869 (10-22-1869) [Ce]
Brinkley, Samuel J. to Serena E. Ozburn 1-13-1876 [Ce]
Brinkley, W. H. to Martha (Mrs.) Harrison 11-7-1871 (11-9-1871) [Ce]
Brinkley, Wm. L. to Marina Fetts 11-14-1857 (11-15-1857) [Ce]
Bristow, William to Martha Cullum 11-14-1859 (11-17-1859) [Ce]
Brooks, Phillip to Caroline Biggs 3-21-1874 (3-22-1874) [Ce]
Brown, Aris to Bettie Pegram 8-29-1863 (8-3?-1863) [Ce]
Brown, Aron to Mariah Chase 2-24-1881 (2-26-1881) B [Ce]
Brown, Avis to M. A. Nelson 2-18-1867 (2-21-1867) [Ce]
Brown, C. F. to Sarah F. Pegram 10-18-1862 [Ce]
Brown, Calvin to Casanda White 7-30-1874 (7-31-1875?) B [Ce]
Brown, Daniel to Mary J. Vick 10-1-1857 [Ce]
Brown, John M. to Harret Reed 9-11-1873 [Ce]
Brown, Joseph to Sarah Nelson 11-18-1871 (11-26-1871) [Ce]
Brown, R. K. to Ellen Newman 11-5-1879 [Ce]
Brown, Richard to Frances Stokes 8-27-1878 B [Ce]
Brown, Robt. to Sayden Easley 4-29-1877 (4-30-1877) B [Ce]
Brown, S. to S. Finch 2-12-1881 (2-14-1881) [Ce]
Brown, S. C. to L. Shrockley 11-1-1862 [Ce]
Brown, Sam to Sarah M. Easley 3-25-1875 B [Ce]
Brown, Sam Y. to R. C. Bell 3-2-1859 (3-3-1859) [Ce]
Brown, W. H. to M. J. Pulley 4-11-1874 (5-16-1874) [Ce]
Brown, William to Missouri J. Russell 1-6-1863 [Ce]
Brown, William to Nancy Crouch 5-4-1871 (5-15-1871) [Ce]
Bryant, Sim to Fannie Hunt 6-24-1871 B [Ce]
Bryant, Wyatt to Lucy Jackson 7-19-1856 (7-25-1856) [Ce]
Buchanan, J. W. to L. L. Curfner 1-8-1881 (1-10-1881) [Ce]
Buckhannan, L. D. to Martha S. Seals 12-9-1874 (12-13-1874) [Ce]
Buckley, W. H. to Mary E. Newland 11-30-1878 (12-1-1878) [Ce]
Burgess, Wm. S. to Nancy C. Bryant 6-5-1869 (6-6-1869) [Ce]
Burton, G. W. to Arrilla Rukes 10-12-1857 (10-13-1857) [Ce]
Bush, Curtis to Margaret Gerdrick 8-1-1878 (8-4-1878) B [Ce]
Butterfield, Andrew to Mary Adline Glasscock 12-30-1878 [Ce]
Cabler, F. H. to Freedonia Stewart 5-1-1858 (5-6-1858) [Ce]
Cagle, Allen to Elizabeth Biggs 1-13-1869 [Ce]
Cagle, C. to E. Simpkins 12-23-1876 (12-24-1876) [Ce]
Cagle, Wm. P. to Mary Binkley 2-3-1876 [Ce]
Cain, A.N. to Victoria Pool 8-18-1859 (8-1?-1859) [Ce]
Cain, J. B. to Melissa A. Hollis 10-22-1870 [Ce]
Cain, James to Loucinda Coleman 1-12-1860 [Ce]
Cain, James H. to Mary J. Thaxton 3-3-1858 (3-4-1858) [Ce]
Cain, John B. to Eliz. Bearden 9-29-1858 [Ce]
Cain, John J. to Verginia T. Pool 12-25-1871 (12-26-1871) [Ce]
Calor, E. R. to Mary E. Stack 9-3-1874 [Ce]
Cam, A. R. to Rosa Pool 10-14-1869 [Ce]
Campbell, James to Mary Templeton 4-21-1864 [Ce]
Canady, Jordan to Manerva Thomas 12-21-1874 B [Ce]
Cantrel, Willie C. to Sary Knight 4-15-1881 [Ce]

Caragen, H. D. to L. L. Stewart 12-18-1880 (12-19-1880) [Ce]
Carney, A. F. to Mary Harper 6-29-1859 [Ce]
Carney, E. B. to Susan Felts 2-1-1865 [Ce]
Carney, E. B. jr. to Eller Simmons 6-9-1873 (6-15-1873) [Ce]
Carney, E. W. to Martha Stewart 11-25-1869 [Ce]
Carney, F. G. to T. J. Moore 10-2-1858 [Ce]
Carney, G. J. to Malvina Bundy? 1-21-1877 [Ce]
Carney, H. J. to S. D. Harris 9-6-1860 [Ce]
Carney, Henry J. to M. Brinkley 12-29-1857 [Ce]
Carney, Hiram B. to Tennie A. Lenox 11-20-1860 [Ce]
Carney, J. H. to S. J. Felts 1-20-1881 [Ce]
Carney, J. H. to Sarah S. Brown 12-31-1872 (1-1-1873) [Ce]
Carney, J. R. P. to P. A. Stewart 12-28-1865 (2-6-1867?) [Ce]
Carney, J. W. to Annie Bell 3-2-1881 [Ce]
Carney, J. W. to Laticia Felts 9-11-1869 [Ce]
Carney, Joshua to S. J. Felts 2-15-1877 [Ce]
Carney, Thomas to Sarah F. Rose 2-3-1872 (2-4-1872) [Ce]
Carney, Thos. J. to Mary L. Abanathy 8-12-1871 [Ce]
Carney, William M. to Lavina Binkley 2-6-1867 (2-7-1867) [Ce]
Carrel, William to Mary E. Ham 12-30-1867 (12-31-1867) [Ce]
Carrol, Wm. to Fannie Jones 3-3-1879 (3-6-1879) [Ce]
Carter, Joseph to Olive W. Hatfield 11-20-1878 B [Ce]
Carter, Joseph to Ollie W. Hatfield 11-30-1878 (no return) [Ce]
Carter, William to Metilda Read 12-22-1866 (12-25-1866) B [Ce]
Casey, William to Rosa Fetts 11-21-1862 [Ce]
Cates, H. C. to Harriet Farmer 11-23-1875 [Ce]
Cato, T. C. to Sarah J. Lenox 12-10-1864 [Ce]
Cearley, S. H. to Rebecca Brown 4-24-1869 (4-29-1869) [Ce]
Cerney, E. B. to Charlott M. Lewis 8-18-1856 (9-25-1856) [Ce]
Chadion, Geo. W. to Alise Carneye 6-13-1878 [Ce]
Chambless, R. to Sarah Knight 10-30-1861 [Ce]
Chambliss, J. W. to Anna R. Mallery 12-20-1876 (12-21-1876) [Ce]
Chambliss, Joseph to Delia Clinard 2-28-1878 (3-1-1878) [Ce]
Chambliss, M. M. to L. A. Read 11-19-1872 (11-20-1872) [Ce]
Chambliss, W. H. to Penola Hyde 12-22-1873 (12-23-1873) [Ce]
Charlton, Moses G. to Margret M. Dunn 2-26-1878 (no return) [Ce]
Cheatham, F. to Elizabeth Cheatham 1-5-1868 B [Ce]
Cherry, W. D. to Sallie E. Newsom 10-18-1867 [Ce]
Clark, Aleck to Martha Bell 10-13-1870 B [Ce]
Clark, Charley to Isabel Shearon 2-2-1874 (3-7-1875?) B [Ce]
Clark, E. J. to Nancy Knight no date (with Jul 1865) [Ce]
Clark, James P. to Amanda Hannah 7-29-1859 (8-3-1859) [Ce]
Clark, John H. to Ludry? G. Harris 12-13-1876 [Ce]
Clark, John H. to Telitha Mays 3-1-1871 [Ce]
Clark, Thos. W. to Mary J. Dunn 11-26-1873 (11-27-1873) [Ce]
Clark, W. C. to Tennie Cullum 7-2-1860 [Ce]
Clark, W. T. to Susan A. Turner 11-6-1863 [Ce]
Claxton, J.L. to E. F. Grove 9-28-1871 [Ce]
Clifton, E. T. to Mary E. Council 5-16-1859 [Ce]
Clifton, S. N. to V. B. Knox 4-18-1866 [Ce]
Clifton, Samuel to Mary M. Adkins 5-10-1856 [Ce]
Clinard, H. M. to Emer Frey 6-3-1879 (6-5-1879) [Ce]
Clinard, Robt. to George Ann Knight 1-9-1877 [Ce]
Cochran, James R. W. to Hulda Boyde 4-9-1881 (4-17-1881) [Ce]

Coffee, Edwin to Larry Lightfoot no date (with 1865) B [Ce]
Collier, Charles to Caroline Collier 5-18-1872 (5-20-1872) B [Ce]
Collier, Phillip to Jenney Robertson 12-24-1873 (12-26-1873) B [Ce]
Collins, Aaron to Gracy Hand 5-25-1867 (5-26-1867) B [Ce]
Collins, D. S. to H. Bames 1-7-1857 (1-8-1857) [Ce]
Collins, Edmond to Mary A. Jones 4-13-1866 (4-14-1866) B [Ce]
Collins, Green M. to Lucinda Collins 3-28-1862 [Ce]
Collins, Jobe to Mary Barton 1-14-1874 (1-16-1874) B [Ce]
Collins, John C. to Amanda Collins 3-20-1860 (3-21-1860) [Ce]
Collins, Joshua to Miley Jones 9-25-1873 B [Ce]
Collins, Robert to Roena Burton 8-13-1879 (8-14-1879) B [Ce]
Colvin, A. J. to Maggie Hale 10-6-1873 (10-9-1873) [Ce]
Cooley, Charles M. to Alice L. Harris 7-24-1874 (7-26-1874) [Ce]
Coon, Isaac A. to Susan A. Nicholson 12-25-1870 (1-1-1871) [Ce]
Copley, A. M. to M. A. Dowlen 11-28-1871 (11-30-1871) [Ce]
Copley, F. M. to Catharine Ross 12-25-1867 [Ce]
Copley, F. M. to Sarah Blain 3-7-1860 (5-16-1860) [Ce]
Corlew, A. P. to Bettie Crumpler 8-31-1881 [Ce]
Corlew, B. J. to M. R. Harris 10-30-1878 [Ce]
Corsan, Samuel H. to Mary M. Porter 2-5-1868 (3-5-1868) [Ce]
Cothren, W. A. to P. M. Lovell 8-22-1861 [Ce]
Cothren, W. A. to Patsey M. Lovell 8-22-1861 [Ce]
Council, D. C. to N. J. Felts 1-23-1871 (1-25-1871) [Ce]
Council, T. D. to Sarah E. Felts 1-7-1867 (1-9-1867) [Ce]
Council, charley to Mollie Batson 2-8-1881 B [Ce]
Cox, S. W. to A. E. Jordan 7-30-1864 [Ce]
Cox, Thomas E. to Nancy Jordan 8-22-1861 [Ce]
Cox, W. J. to Caroline Hicks 4-24-1878 [Ce]
Cozo?, James E. to Mattie A. Pardue 11-16-1868 (11-17-1868) [Ce]
Craig, G. W. to Elizabeth T. Setton 6-22-1878 (no return) [Ce]
Craighead, James to Florrence Willis 4-14-1876 (4-16-1876) B [Ce]
Crall, Andrew J. to Nancy E. Jones 9-25-1857 [Ce]
Crantz, A. G. to H. C. Miles 9-18-1870 [Ce]
Crantz, A. J. to M. E. Gibbs 3-23-1867 (3-27-1867) [Ce]
Crantz, Robert to Marina Cagle 1-25-1866 [Ce]
Crawford, H. E. to Chairity M. Elliott 11-22-1866 [Ce]
Creech, William to Mary A. Andrews 3-21-1861 [Ce]
Crenshaw, James C. to Mortica E. Talley 1-11-1861 [Ce]
Crenshaw, Jas. C. to M. E. Talley 1-11-1861 [Ce]
Crocker, A. W. to Susan Mays 11-14-1861 [Ce]
Cross, Wm. B. to Tennessee Barton 8-14-1856 [Ce]
Crotzer, W. H. to Korrener? C. Nickolson 2-10-1868 (2-11-1868) [Ce]
Crouch, A. J. to Lizzie Jordan 12-5-1874 [Ce]
Crouch, Thomas J. to Rebecca Jordan 6-28-1859 [Ce]
Crouch, W. J. to Lucada Hale 9-21-1861 (9-22-1861) [Ce]
Crouch, W. S. to Mary Lovell 12-24-1874 (12-28-1874) [Ce]
Crumpler, M. J. to Dora E. Crumpler 3-17-1863 [Ce]
Crunk, Walton to Sarah Morris 12-5-1868 (12-6-1868) [Ce]
Cullum, D. C. to Mary E. Hunt 12-14-1859 (12-29-1860?) [Ce]
Cullum, Daid C. to Susan R. Felts 8-21-1867 [Ce]
Cullum, E. G. to Elizabeth Work 3-2-1868 [Ce]
Cullum, L. H. to N. E. Hooper 2-21-1867 (2-22-1867) [Ce]
Cullum, Thomas H. to Irene Lovell 11-18-1869 [Ce]
Cullum, W. L. to E. C. Work 3-2-1868 (3-3-1868) [Ce]

Cullum, William L. to M. J. Henderson 3-6-1857 (3-15-1857) [Ce]
Cullun, G. F. to Mollie Lovell 12-30-1874 [Ce]
Cuningham, Granvill to Emer Tally 2-2-1872 (2-4-1872) B [Ce]
Curtis, John G. to Martha A. Miles 10-25-1858 (10-27-1858) [Ce]
Curtis, Marion to Martha A. Neighbors 5-30-1870 (6-11-1870) [Ce]
Daniel, S. to Bettie Anderson 6-30-1877 (7-1-1877) B [Ce]
Daniel, W. H. to M. P. Hagwood 12-15-1860 (12-16-1860) [Ce]
Dann, S. K. to Lucada Fulghum 5-11-1865 (5-18-1865) [Ce]
Darden, W. J. to E. C. Gardner 11-10-1866 [Ce]
Darrow, Albert to Elizabeth Durard 4-24-1867 (4-25-1867) [Ce]
Darrow, C. C. to E. C. Boyd 12-24-1877 [Ce]
Darrow, G. W. to Nancy Simpson 9-21-1875 [Ce]
Darrow, Isaac to Mary Newman 5-15-1872 (5-16-1872) [Ce]
Darrow, J. D. to Lutitia T. Carpenter 10-14-1874 [Ce]
Davis, B. M. to Ann Smith 11-17-1865 [Ce]
Davis, J. B. to Eller Shearon 9-1-1877 (9-2-1877) [Ce]
Davis, James to T. E. Gower 1-12-1858 (1-13-1858) [Ce]
Davis, Johnson to Judith Williams 1-31-1880 B [Ce]
Davis, Lemuel to Mary Clifton 1-5-1870 (1-6-1870) [Ce]
Davis, William to Elizabeth Hudgens 6-1-1874 (6-2-1874) [Ce]
Deal, W. W. to Fannie F. Scott 5-11-1861 [Ce]
Deal, W. W. to Fannie F. Scott 5-11-1861 [Ce]
Deal, William T. to Mary Deal 1-16-1875 [Ce]
Deal, William W. to Lueaser Wynn 9-23-1872 (9-24-1872) [Ce]
Dean, John A. to L. J. Dunn 5-28-1873 (5-29-1873) [Ce]
Demumbra, Benjamin to Sarah Morris 10-14-1876 (10-15-1876) [Ce]
Demumbra, D. H. to Rebecca J. Nichols 12-23-1872 (11-13-1872) [Ce]
Demumbra, J. S. to Sarah A. Biggs 8-7-1874 (8-8-1874) [Ce]
Demumbra, J. W. to Elisa A. Cagle 1-7-1873 (1-9-1873) [Ce]
Demumbra, J. W. to Martha Binkley 6-16-1876 (6-18-1876) [Ce]
Demumbra, John B. to Catharine Brinkley 3-17-1860 (3-18-1860) [Ce]
Demumbra, R. W. to Mary Boyd 6-24-1871 [Ce]
Demumbra, S. H. to Mildred Fraley 12-22-1877 (12-23-1877) [Ce]
Denney, William to Mary A. Fielder 7-19-1862 (7-24-1862) [Ce]
Denny, A. J. to Josephine Williams 8-4-1869 [Ce]
Dickerson, Lewis to A. Demumbra 5-15-1876 [Ce]
Dickerson, O. H. to Mary T. Bennett 12-2-1858 (12-5-1858) [Ce]
Dickerson, Silas to Harriet Darden 5-25-1867 (6-1-1867) B [Ce]
Dickerson, Thomas to Harriet Shumake 6-24-1870 (6-26-1870) [Ce]
Dickins?, Thomas to Mary Ivy 2-5-1867 (2-6-1867) [Ce]
Dillingham, B. C. to Nancy E. Godsey 7-29-1857 [Ce]
Dillingham, George J. to Susie A. Whitfield 12-29-1878 [Ce]
Dillingham, James to Annie T. Reggan 1-20-1878 [Ce]
Dillingham, John N. to Sarah Jane Hain 2-9-1871 (2-23-1871) [Ce]
Dillingham, W. J. to Nannie E. Stinnett 10-25-1875 (10-27-1875) [Ce]
Doke, Thomas A. to Elizabeth O. Miles 11-3-1873 (11-9-1873) [Ce]
Donil?, Stephen to Samuel Eller Young 6-25-1867 (7-4-1867) [Ce]
Dortch, John J. to Eveline V. Ross 5-23-1868 (5-24-1868) [Ce]
Douglas, Andrew K. to Virgina D. Felts 10-18-1878 (10-19-1878) [Ce]
Douglas, James R. to Susan E. Greene 5-19-1860 (5-20-1860) [Ce]
Douglas, R. E. to C. O. Bell 9-27-1860 (9-28-1860) [Ce]
Dowlen, Andrew to Mahala Mallory 7-28-1879 B [Ce]
Dowlen, Andrew to Mary Woodson 7-4-1866 (7-8-1866) B [Ce]
Dowlen, Andrew to Tempy Washington 2-17-1868 (2-23-1868) B [Ce]

Dowlen, Ben to Arena Williams 1-10-1879 B [Ce]
Dowlen, Charles to Luella L. Ralls 3-24-1871 (3-28-1871) [Ce]
Dowlen, David to Nancy Wilson 1-28-1874 (1-29-1874) B [Ce]
Dowlen, George to Sarah A. Knight 7-14-1862 [Ce]
Dowlen, Henry to Eliza Wilson 8-31-1874 B [Ce]
Dowlen, Henry to S. E. Fortune 2-21-1866 [Ce]
Dowlen, S. to C. J. Hudgens 1-15-1870 (1-20-1870) [Ce]
Dowlen, W. R. to N. E. Simmons 12-9-1878 (12-11-1878) [Ce]
Dowlen, William to Louisa J. Fortane 12-24-1861 [Ce]
Dowlin, Ben to Ann Williams 1-10-1879 B [Ce]
Dozier, A. J. to Mary E. Kerby 7-22-1876 (7-23-1876) [Ce]
Dozier, A. P. jr. to A. J. Hooper 12-20-1880 (12-21-1880) [Ce]
Dozier, H. to Susan Crockett 12-27-1876 B [Ce]
Dozier, H. C. to Mary E. Riggan 8-12-1876 [Ce]
Dozier, Henry to Julia Page 10-19-1869 (10-20-1869) B [Ce]
Dozier, J. W. to Jenne Hooper 10-25-1862 (10-29-1862) [Ce]
Dozier, James A. to Mary E. Simmons 1-8-1874 [Ce]
Dozier, Joseph to F. A. Riggan 1-23-1879 (1-26-1879) [Ce]
Dozier, P. H. to Susan E. Hooper 10-8-1872 (10-9-1872) [Ce]
Dozier, Thos. J. to Ann E. Harris 10-5-1872 [Ce]
Dozier, W. C. to Toonothy? Story 10-21-1875 [Ce]
Dozier, W. N. to S. T. Lovell 1-10-1865 [Ce]
Drake, Albin G. to Adaline Martin 7-14-1856 [Ce]
Drake, Joseph D. to Mary E. Drake 4-15-1865 [Ce]
Drake, Lewis to Charlotte Woodward 12-24-1871 (1-21-1872) B [Ce]
Duke, John M. to Henrietta L. Gupton 3-8-1869 [Ce]
Dunkin, Taylor to Martha Shelton 12-30-1871 B [Ce]
Dunn, George to Dicy Gray 3-22-1874 (3-26-1874) B [Ce]
Dunn, Gustavus to Martha E. Turner 11-6-1872 [Ce]
Dunn, Samuel H. to Julia F. Lee 12-13-1859 [Ce]
Dunn, Samuel H. to Julia F. Lee 12-13-1859 (12-29-1859) [Ce]
Dunn, Wm. T. to Alice G. Riggan 9-23-1876 (9-26-1876) [Ce]
Dwiss?, John T. to Sarah Jarrel 6-2-1863 [Ce]
Dye, Moses to Elizabeth Wilson 1-18-1866 (6?-18-1866) B [Ce]
Dyer, Edmond to Malinda Dyer 7-27-1865 B [Ce]
Dyer, G. W. to Ida M. Dismukes 3-4-1880 [Ce]
Eakin, David A. to Margaret L. Ham 12-16-1875 (12-23-1875) [Ce]
Eastridge, ---san to M. J. Perry 11-1-1878 (11-10-1878) [Ce]
Eastridge, Timothy to Sarah Read 7-13-1871 (7-16-1871) [Ce]
Eatherly, J. M. to Launa J. Work 10-21-1871 (10-25-1871) [Ce]
Eatherly, James to Nannie Miles 3-6-1878 [Ce]
Eatherly, W. A. to S. E. Edwards 1-21-1869 (1-28-1869) [Ce]
Eatherly, William A. to Georgia Brinkley 1-15-1874 [Ce]
Eatherly, Wm. to Lucy A. Sanders 2-19-1867 (2-21-1867) [Ce]
Edger, Wm. to O. Nanney 3-24-1880 (3-25-1880) [Ce]
Edgin, Jno. A. to Narcissa Batsen 6-6-1877 (6-8-1877) [Ce]
Edgin, John A. to Emily Alley 9-?-1858 (9-29-1858) [Ce]
Edgin, W. A. to L. A. Binkley 1-18-1865 [Ce]
Edward, W. J. to Sis? Gower 10-22-1878 (10-31-1878) [Ce]
Edwards, B. J. to H. A. Bawsel 3-3-1873 (3-4-1873) [Ce]
Edwards, Bursell to Mary Jane Brown 7-17-1868 (7-18-1868 [Ce]
Edwards, Jessee T. to Mary Y. Lenox 11-6-1866 (11-13-1866) [Ce]
Edwards, Joshua to Arminty Hudgens 3-25-1870 B [Ce]
Edwards, O. to Sarah A. Smith 8-18-1863 [Ce]

Edwards, Rufus to Sarah Eatherly 1-30-1863 (2-1-1863) [Ce]
Edwards, W. E. to V. E. Edwards 1-3-1876 [Ce]
Edwards, Wesley to Amanda Cato? 12-25-1871 B [Ce]
Edwards, Wesley to Lucy A. Hudgens 11-15-1876 (11-18-1876) B [Ce]
Eleazer, John L.? to Martha M. Weakley 1-20-1868 (1-22-1868) [Ce]
Eleazier, S. G. to S. O. Woodward 5-1-1858 (5-5-1858) [Ce]
Eleazor, Geo. A. to Luan Collins 8-24-1860 (8-26-1860) [Ce]
Elliott, D. J. to Katie Stack 12-8-1877 (12-13-1877) [Ce]
Elliott, George M. to Priscilla Thompson 9-3-1858 (9-4-1858) [Ce]
Elliott, Henry to Racheal Majors 12-25-1873 (12-26-1873) B [Ce]
Elliott, John M. to Eliz. A. McCarrol 9-4-1867 (8-5-1867) [Ce]
Elliott, Stephen A. M. to Margret J. McCarrall 3-11-1870 [Ce]
Elliott, T. to Sarah M. Vanvolkenberg 2-26-1862 (3-2-1862) [Ce]
Elliott, Taylor to Permeld Barton 12-25-1872 (12-26-1872) B [Ce]
Ellis, E. S. to M. E. Lawrence 5-26-1877 (5-27-1877) [Ce]
Ellis, Felix to Ferebee Nichols 4-9-1872 (4-10-1872) B [Ce]
Ellis, G. F. to Nancy J. Knox 12-27-1866 (12-31-1866) [Ce]
Elrod, James to Susan Burrow 7-27-1865 B [Ce]
Evans, D. A. to S. E. Edwards 12-21-1868 (12-22-1868) [Ce]
Evans, E. E. to G. A. Adams 10-2-1879 [Ce]
Evans, J. J. to Josephine Moore 4-26-1869 (4-29-1869) [Ce]
Everett, J. J. to Emily R. Sander 1-27-1869 (1-28-1869) [Ce]
Everett, James to Mary Williams 6-18-1874 B [Ce]
Everett, Pike to Narcissa Hall 9-24-1868 [Ce]
Evilcizer, John to Martha A. Pace 6-30-1869 (7-3-1869) [Ce]
Fambrough, John T. to Mehaly C. Nichols 7-22-1868 (7-23-1868) [Ce]
Farley, Shadrick to Susan Jordan 11-19-1866 B [Ce]
Farmbrugh, Robert to Mossa Farmbrough 4-16-1857 [Ce]
Farmer, C. R. to M. W. McDaniel 3-29-1879 (3-30-1879) [Ce]
Farmer, James to Angeline Ford 7-4-1866 [Ce]
Farmer, John to Lilly Clark 3-12-1881 (3-13-1881) [Ce]
Farmer, Thomas J. to Mary Binkley 10-20-1871 (10-22-1871) [Ce]
Farmer, W. H. to Sarah B. Durham 11-5-1869 [Ce]
Farmer, W. T. to Mary L. Cochran 8-7-1876 (8-17-1876) [Ce]
Farner, Joh to AlliceM. Noe 4-8-1871 (4-9-1871) [Ce]
Felts, C. R. to Mary Keeler 12-20-1875 (12-22-1875) [Ce]
Felts, J. A. to Lou Binkley 6-14-1879 [Ce]
Felts, J. H. to Anna J. Buckley 3-21-1878 (3-24-1878) [Ce]
Felts, Maxo? to Maggie J. Carney 11-25-1878 (11-26-1878) [Ce]
Felts, R. J. to M. L. Gleeves 6-28-1880 [Ce]
Felts, R. R. to C. H. Williams 11-15-1878 (11-17-1878) [Ce]
Felts, R. W. to Martha Harris 7-27-1864 [Ce]
Felts, Rufus M. to Perlina F. Chambliss 3-31-1869 (4-1-1869) [Ce]
Felts, Wm. R. to Margret E. Henderson 12-24-1870 (12-25-1870) [Ce]
Ferebee, Charles to Tennessee Beck 12-18-1871 (12-23-1871) B [Ce]
Fetts, D. J. to H. J. Binkley 1-4-1858 [Ce]
Fetts, David J. to H. J. Brinkley 1-4-1858 [Ce]
Fetts, E. W. to C. H. Miles 11-21-1857 [Ce]
Fielder, B. F. to M. J. Pinson 4-28-1869 (4-29-1869) [Ce]
Fielder, J. T. to Nannie A. Eatherley 12-16-1878 (12-19-1878) [Ce]
Fielder, J. W. to Netta Frazier 2-5-1877 (2-8-1877) [Ce]
Fielder, John G. to M. J. Denney 1-6-1858 [Ce]
Fields, James W. to Marth E. Jones 6-9-1862 (6-12-1862) [Ce]
Fikes, Benjamin to Mattie Watson 3-22-1871 B [Ce]

Finch, George P. to Eury F. Osborne 11-5-1877 (11-13-1877) [Ce]
Finley, Berge to Polly Clark 4-19-1867 B [Ce]
Fitts, Hiram D. to Malinda Casey 5-27-1857 [Ce]
Fizer, S. W. to F. P. Morris 1-6-1872 (1-7-1872) [Ce]
Fleaney, Robert to Mary J. Felts 1-23-1877 (1-24-1877) [Ce]
Flintoff, H. C. to Alta Mallory 12-26-1874 (12-28-1874) [Ce]
Follis, Dick to Nancy Perdue 1-13-1875 (1-14-1875) B [Ce]
Follis, W. F. to M. A. Brinkley 3-7-1861 [Ce]
Ford, Franklin to Mary E. Burkley 12-24-1877 (12-25-1877) [Ce]
Fordner, Thomas to Mahala Shearin 3-11-1876 B [Ce]
Forrest, Wm. H. H. to Mary Atkison 1-8-1876 B [Ce]
Fort, W. R. to Mary Pennington 7-4-1872 [Ce]
Forte?, George M. to Eliza White 8-3-1880 (8-4-1880) B [Ce]
Foster, John to Sarah J. Bidwell 9-28-1867 (10-12-1867) B [Ce]
Fox, H. C. to Elizabeth K. Walker 1-28-1873 (1-29-1873) [Ce]
Fox?, G. R. to Sarah A. Allers 10-11-1876 (10-12-1876) [Ce]
Frazier, B. H. to Nancy Bearden 1-12-1858 (1-14-1858) [Ce]
Frazier, Charles to Mandy Oakley 7-29-1880 (7-30-1880) B [Ce]
Frazier, G. H. to Lucy Jane Gupton 1-7-1880 [Ce]
Frazier, T. B. to Ida A. King 12-19-1879 (12-21-1879) [Ce]
Frazier, William to Jeraline Williams 11-19-1877 (11-22-1877) B [Ce]
Frazier, William to L. A. Hunter 11-15-1865 [Ce]
Freeman, R. S. to N. E. Shaw 10-16-1878 (10-17-1878) [Ce]
Frey, W. F. to A. H. Felts 1-10-1874 (1-13-1874) [Ce]
Frey, W.F. to Huldah Dowlen 10-15-1856 [Ce]
Frey?, William to Martha Harris 7-4-1867 (7-7-1867) B [Ce]
Friendsley, John F. to Unis C. Carney 2-3-1873 (2-7-1873) [Ce]
Friendsly, T. R. to Martha E. Davis 7-26-1876 (7-27-1876) [Ce]
Fulghum, James H. to E. J. Ussery 7-29-1857 (10-4-1857) [Ce]
Fulghum, James H. to Mary A. Ussery 5-22-1865 [Ce]
Fulghum, W. J. to M. C. Fulgham 8-7-1876 (8-16-1876) [Ce]
Gallaher, W. A. to Eliza Buckley 10-9-1875 (10-10-1875) [Ce]
Galligan, L. to June Mathas 10-25-1876 [Ce]
Galligan, Patrick to Lydia A. Perry 5-14-1866 (5-13?-1866) [Ce]
Galloway, Alexander to Mary D. Davis 12-25-1874 [Ce]
Gardner, J. P. to Elenor Drake 1-2-1860 [Ce]
Garland, James to Eliza Fletcher 7-23-1867 (7-24-1867) [Ce]
Garland, S. J. to Sarah E. Hambrick 12-30-1875 [Ce]
Garrett, Thomas to Nancy Woodson 2-12-1869 (2-13-1869) B [Ce]
Garrett, W. L. to Roena P. Mallory 2-9-1857 (2-15-1857) [Ce]
Garton, Mark to Elizabeth Greer 1-6-1857 (1-7-1857) [Ce]
Garvits?, Robt. S. to Lucy Cole 3-9-1881 (3-11-1881) B [Ce]
Gatewood, Jos. to Emma Jenkins 12-3-1880 (12-5-1880) [Ce]
Gattis, Joseph to Mary More 9-5-1867 [Ce]
Gent, W. H. H. to Evaline Stewart 11-10-1858 (11-11-1858) [Ce]
Gibbs, John T. to Loucinda Fielder 1-30-1879 [Ce]
Girard, J. L. to Roena Felts 8-6-1872 (8-7-1872) [Ce]
Glass, Sam F. to M. E. Barclift 5-30-1860 [Ce]
Gleason, William J. to M. M. Dunn 3-30-1868 (4-7-1868) [Ce]
Gleaves, W. D. to Louisa Lowe 1-2-1860 (1-4-1860) [Ce]
Godsey, G. to E. McCormack 7-20-857 [Ce]
Goodlett, A. G. to Sarah D. Hooper 9-6-1863 [Ce]
Goodwin, William to Susan C. Cagle 4-14-1857 (4-16-1857) [Ce]
Gorden, Robert to Mary Robertson 6-1-1872 (6-2-1872) B [Ce]

Gossett, W. T. to M. A. Hunter 1-4-1859 (1-6-1859) [Ce]
Gower, A. M. to Nancy Martin 10-5-1859 [Ce]
Gower, Ehud? to Elizabeth Jordan 7-10-1866 [Ce]
Gower, G. F. to V. L. Gray 1-7-1871 (1-11-1871) [Ce]
Gower, W. T. to Cornelius T. Nichols 10-16-1876 (10-19-1876) [Ce]
Grant, Hardy to Mary Barton 4-6-1872 B [Ce]
Grant, Joseph to M. J. Morris 11-19-1859 (11-26-1859) [Ce]
Gray, J. J. to Henrietta Manwarin 11-8-1879 (11-9-1879) [Ce]
Gray, Thos. L. to Ann M. Bright 11-30-1857 (12-9-1857) [Ce]
Gray, W. J. to S. A. Alley 2-3-1858 (2-4-1858) [Ce]
Gray, Walter G. to Elizabeth Read 8-11-1880 (8-12-1880) [Ce]
Gray, Washington to Medora Harper 3-20-1880 (3-21-1880) [Ce]
Green, Johnerthan to Eliza Farmer 3-15-1869 (3-16-1869) [Ce]
Green, L. L. to Mary E. Walker 12-28-1865 [Ce]
Greene, G. jr. to Cornelia Russell 9-16-1872 [Ce]
Greene, John G. to Rebecca E. Tymms 8-18-1860 (8-19-1860) [Ce]
Greene, N. L. to Martha J. Blankenship 10-19-1874 [Ce]
Greer, Alfred to Harriet Hudelston 4-1-1878 B [Ce]
Greer, Cezar to Caty Hannah 2-16-1871 B [Ce]
Greer, Genrl. J. to Margret Henry 2-8-1870 [Ce]
Greer, Green to Bettie Ussery 11-29-1876 (11-30-1876) B [Ce]
Greer, James W. to Mary E. Jones 12-16-1867 (12-19-1867) [Ce]
Greer, John H. W. to Emma M. Bagwell 1-25-1875 (1-26-1875) [Ce]
Greer, Luke to Ellen Dunn 1-19-1874 (1-25-1874) B [Ce]
Greer, Nathan G. B. to Harriett E. Henry 1-31-1881 (2-3-1881) [Ce]
Greer, Silas to Susa Bledsoe 10-8-1866 (11-6-1866) [Ce]
Greer, Wm. C. to Nannie G. Helton 7-24-1877 (7-25-1877) [Ce]
Grey, L. C. to F. Sheron 4-28-1877 (4-29-1877) [Ce]
Grimes, C. D. to M. F. Grine 11-27-1876 [Ce]
Grimes, F. to Eliz. King 12-31-1857 [Ce]
Groves, H. J. to Mallinda Christy 10-14-1878 (10-20-1878) [Ce]
Guin, G. to N. E. Dunlap 1-5-1857 [Ce]
Gunter, William J. to Victoria A. Beach 12-18-1879 [Ce]
Gupton, Franklin to Martha Jones 3-8-1881 (3-9-1881) [Ce]
Gupton, J. W. to Henrietta Gupton 10-28-1873 (10-29-1873) [Ce]
Gupton, James H. to M. T. Dowling 10-25-1860 [Ce]
Gupton, John to Geriline Frazier 11-3-1879 (11-6-1879) [Ce]
Gupton, John J. to Martha J. Gupton 5-9-1871 (5-10-1871) [Ce]
Gupton, Thomas W. to Nancy Pinson 9-13-1866 (9-16-1866) [Ce]
Gupton, William to Sarah E. Bell 10-14-1873 (10-13?-1873) [Ce]
Guthrie, John to Nancy Blane 1-16-1867 (1-17-1867) [Ce]
Hagewood, B. H. to Telulia J. Patterson 12-19-1877 (12-20-1877) [Ce]
Hagewood, C. J. to Viola L. Smith 12-20-1873 (12-30-1873) [Ce]
Hagewood, J. A. to Cerdely A. Hagewood 8-4-1876 (8-27-1876) [Ce]
Hagewood, J. W. D. to Mary D. Hagewood 10-6-1879 (10-30-1879) [Ce]
Hagewood, Jesse B. to Ida Monroe 12-24-1874 [Ce]
Hagewood, John A. to Elizabeth Mecaba 12-31-1856 (12-30?-1856) [Ce]
Hagewood, T. J. to L. C. Smith 6-10-1873 [Ce]
Hagewood, W. to Lyddia Hagewood 4-15-1878 (no return) [Ce]
Haggard, Samuel H. to Nancy Ford 11-14-1866 (11-15-1866) [Ce]
Hale, Alexander to Darcus Cox 6-20-1868 B [Ce]
Hale, Alexr. to Chaerty? Bell 9-3-1866 (9-6-1866) B [Ce]
Hale, B. B. to Martha Jones 2-26-1877 (2-28-1877) [Ce]
Hale, Jerry to Delila Butler 1-11-1867 (1-13-1867) B [Ce]

Hale, John C. to M. C. Hooper 6-5-1858 (6-6-1858) [Ce]
Hale, Stephen B. to Permelia McDaniel 3-20-1857 (3-22-1857) [Ce]
Hale, Wm. J. to Margret Harris 9-28-1869 (10-3-1869) [Ce]
Hall, C. C. to Annie H. Story 11-5-1878 [Ce]
Hall, Eliza to Mary a. Naney 7-19-1862 (7-23-1862) [Ce]
Hall, John B. to Harriet Woodward 9-14-1873 (9-23-1873) [Ce]
Hall, William H. to Sarah H. Pace 10-6-1870 (10-7-1870) [Ce]
Halley, John S. to Martha Mays 3-28-1857 (3-29-1857) [Ce]
Ham, J. D. to M. E. Dillingham 5-29-1871 (6-1-1871) [Ce]
Ham, Jessie W. to Elizabeth Funch 12-13-1873 (12-18-1873) [Ce]
Ham, Wm. J. to Ruth Caral 12-4-1869 (12-5-1869) [Ce]
Hameris?, John H. to Geneva Roope 3-23-1867 [Ce]
Hamilton, Andrew to Sarah A. Owen 12-12-1876 [Ce]
Hamilton, Carroll to Adaline Chase 9-22-1877 B [Ce]
Hamilton, James R. to Susanah Allen 10-1-1874 [Ce]
Hamlin, Jerry to Mandy Curtis 12-25-1878 (12-26-1878) B [Ce]
Hampton, Jas. W. to Martha J. Christy 5-5-1879 (5-7-1879) [Ce]
Hampton, Joseph to Mary F. Raymer 12-15-1877 (no return) [Ce]
Hampton, Y. J. to Martha L. Hollis 2-28-1878 (3-1-1878) [Ce]
Hand, Joseph to Eller D. Bobbitt 2-27-1878 [Ce]
Hannah, B. F. to Annie Scott 1-19-1867 [Ce]
Hannah, Benjamin F. to Annie Scott 4-4-1868 (4-5-1868) [Ce]
Hardeman, James to Hettie Robinson 9-11-1876 B [Ce]
Haris, M. to Mary Stewart 12-16-1867 (12-18-1867) [Ce]
Harper, C. A. to Louisa McCormack 5-10-1864 [Ce]
Harper, Doc to Fannie Ray 4-8-1881 (4-10-1881) [Ce]
Harper, William to Lucy Stringfellow 12-21-1871 (12-29-1871) [Ce]
Harrel, Jessee to Narcissa McCormack no date (with Jan 1873) [Ce]
Harrington, G. W. to Mary H. Harrington 10-20-1858 (10-21-1858) [Ce]
Harrington, George to Mollie Perry 5-30-1872 (6-2-1872) [Ce]
Harrington, James to Frances T. Knight 2-5-1878 [Ce]
Harrington, Larkin to Jane Litle 4-11-1870 [Ce]
Harris, Alexander to Patsey Sawyer 4-4-1880 B [Ce]
Harris, Amos Marcus to Lougenia Lay 12-13-1878 (12-15-1878) [Ce]
Harris, B. F. to Sally Pool 9-21-1880 [Ce]
Harris, Charles to Rutha Chase 12-5-1868 (12-13-1868) B [Ce]
Harris, E. F. to Cresia Nichols 2-8-1866 [Ce]
Harris, Edwin to Alice Hooper 11-30-1877 (12-2-1877) B [Ce]
Harris, Eli to Fredonia Nicholson 7-31-1857 (8-3-1857) [Ce]
Harris, G. B. to F. H. Fetts 10-21-1858 [Ce]
Harris, G. W. to Elvira Casey 10-4-1860 (12-10-1860) [Ce]
Harris, Geo. W. to Emily R. Shearon 7-9-1861 [Ce]
Harris, George to Cherry Brown 12-18-1874 B [Ce]
Harris, George to Milley Sewell 12-23-1874 [Ce]
Harris, J. W. to F. E. Williams 10-4-1880 (10-5-1880) [Ce]
Harris, Jas. C. to Mary C. Walker 2-1-1876 (2-3-1876) [Ce]
Harris, Joel J. to Rosa C. Lanier 8-5-1868 (8-6-1868) [Ce]
Harris, John to Margaret Anderson 7-19-1871 (7-22-1871) [Ce]
Harris, John to Sarah Knox 4-14-1879 (4-17-1879) [Ce]
Harris, Joseph to Georg A. Nichols 9-6-1870 (9-7-1870) [Ce]
Harris, Mathew T. to Ellen Nichols 8-21-1867 (8-22-1867) [Ce]
Harris, N. B. to Mersie Johnson 12-12-1873 (12-14-1873) [Ce]
Harris, Newsom to Sarah Stewart 4-24-1858 (4-25-1858) [Ce]
Harris, R. T. to Mary Shearon 6-5-1880 (6-6-1880) [Ce]

Harris, Rufus to Luvenia Harris 12-28-1871 (12-29-1871) [Ce]
Harris, S. C. to Lucinda Harris 3-25-1861 (3-28-1861) [Ce]
Harris, T. R. to N. J. Teasley 1-7-1876 (1-9-1876) [Ce]
Harris, Tillman to Kitty Walker 1-6-1868 (6?-7-1868) B [Ce]
Harris, W. H. to Martha J. Sanders 8-21-1869 (8-22-1869) [Ce]
Harris, W. M. to Beesty? F. Douglass 12-18-1871 (12-19-1871) [Ce]
Harris, W. R. to Drebra Head 4-30-1872 (5-2-1872) [Ce]
Harris, Willis to Amy Council 11-28-1867 B [Ce]
Harris, Wm. W. to Rosa E. Darrow 5-18-1874 (6-7-1874) [Ce]
Harris, Z. T. to Luvenia Sanders 1-8-1874 (1-11-1874) [Ce]
Harrison, Allen J. to Mattie A. Gupton 9-13-1861 [Ce]
Haskins, C. H. to Frances C. Mays 9-17-1862 (10-26-1862) [Ce]
Hasley, George B. to Nancy C. F. Hefner 9-1-1865 [Ce]
Hatcher, B. H. to M. B. Dill 1-21-1858 [Ce]
Hawkins, Benjamin C. to Mary E. Thompson 2-20-1861 [Ce]
Head, Edward Ned to Sallie Stewart 3-22-1873 B [Ce]
Head, F. P. to L. E. Innman 11-3-1873 [Ce]
Head, George to Nancy Hesbey? 4-21-1881 B [Ce]
Head, J. H. to Dibra Binkley 11-4-1867 (11-7-1867) [Ce]
Head, James to Evaline Watson 3-22-1871 B [Ce]
Head, W. C. to Sarah A. Simpkins 11-15-1875 (11-18-1875) [Ce]
Head, Wesley to Bettie Power 7-17-1879 B [Ce]
Head, Wm. C. to Mary E. Walker 9-9-1869 (9-15-1869) [Ce]
Heflin, Q. E. to M. M. Smith 1-29-1874 [Ce]
Henderson, J. P. B. to Margret Simmons 7-4-1859 (7-6-1859) [Ce]
Henderson, John Y. to Arlena Jenett 12-19-1856 (12-17?-1856) [Ce]
Henderson, William to Adaline Nicholson 7-6-1868 (7-11-1868) B [Ce]
Henn?, Thos. S. to Susanah E. Bennett 12-22-1857 [Ce]
Henry, Oliver to Rosanah Shelton 3-3-1871 B [Ce]
Herrin, H. A. to Sallie A. Henry 7-10-1876 (7-16-1876) [Ce]
Hewitt, Edward to Augusta H. Balthrop 10-19-1874 (10-20-1874) [Ce]
Heyde, Jessee to Racheal Craighead 2-21-1877 (2-26-1877) B [Ce]
Hicks, James D. to Anna R. Felts 10-10-1867 [Ce]
Hicks, L. H. to Virginia L. Buckley 10-21-1872 (10-23-1872) [Ce]
Hicks, M. V. to Nancy D.? Hooper 1-1-1869 [Ce]
Hicks, M. V. B. to L. Lovell 2-23-1861 (2-24-1861) [Ce]
Hicks, W. H. to Martha E. Slump 8-4-1880 [Ce]
Higgins, J. A. to Katie Russell 2-15-1875 [Ce]
Higgins, John to Dolla Haguewood 4-7-1879 (4-16-1879) [Ce]
Hiland, A. P. to Indiana Johnson 9-3-1877 (8?-5-1877) [Ce]
Hiland, A. P. to Martha Everett 11-22-1866 [Ce]
Hiland, G. W. to Fredonia Mickle 12-14-1874 (12-15-1874) [Ce]
Hill, John D. to E.J. Daily 8-3-1863 [Ce]
Hogan, J. W. to Car Weakley 12-29-1856 (12-31-1856) [Ce]
Hoge, Andrew to Catharine Lovell 10-9-1862 (10-15-1862) [Ce]
Hogins, Edward to Caroline White 10-15-1868 B [Ce]
Hollensworth, Simon to Susan Shelton 12-7-1878 (12-8-1878) B [Ce]
Hollis, Alva to Mattie McCormac 2-17-1881 (2-20-1881) [Ce]
Hollis, C. J. to Emma Nanney 1-19-1880 [Ce]
Hollis, James S. to Susan J. Brinkley 2-27-1861 (2-28-1861) [Ce]
Hollis, John to Jemima Thaxton 4-15-1859 (4-17-1859) [Ce]
Hollis, Johnathan to Elizabeth Johnson 9-24-1872 [Ce]
Holt, Henry to Emer Charlton 7-6-1878 (7-8-1878) B [Ce]
Holt, Henry to Mary Ann Perry 2-13-1875 (2-14-1875) [Ce]

Holt, Martin to Malinda Thompson 10-13-1873 B [Ce]
Holt, William to Judith A. Pegram 1-30-1864 (2-4-1864) [Ce]
Hoobury, Wm. C. to Nanny Lovell 10-10-1874 (10-6?-1874) [Ce]
Hooper, C. S. to Mary A. Riggin 9-25-1865 (9-27-1865) [Ce]
Hooper, D. W. to Jemima Grown 12-1-1866 (12-9-1866) [Ce]
Hooper, David C. to S. A. Dozier 8-27-1857 [Ce]
Hooper, F. M. to Elizabeth Lovell 12-8-1874 (12-9-1874) [Ce]
Hooper, F. M. to Samuel Ellen Jordan 10-13-1874 [Ce]
Hooper, J. B. to M. J. Riggin 9-15-1865 (9-27-1865) [Ce]
Hooper, J. O. to M. C. Cullum 12-8-1865 [Ce]
Hooper, J. O. R. to Anna J. Rogers 9-18-1866 [Ce]
Hooper, J.M. to Mary E. Ussery 12-22-1866 (12-26-1866) [Ce]
Hooper, James to Priscilla Hale 4-25-1878 (4-28-1878) [Ce]
Hooper, James N. to Ann Crouch 10-8-1872 (10-9-1872) [Ce]
Hooper, Jerry to Sallie Ewing 7-29-1873 [Ce]
Hooper, Jessee to Nancy A. Dozier 9-20-1861 (9-22-1861) [Ce]
Hooper, John to A. R. Williams 4-29-1863 [Ce]
Hooper, John T. to Rebecca Majors 11-14-1859 (11-16-1859) [Ce]
Hooper, Jordan to Elizabeth Ferrile 5-24-1856 [Ce]
Hooper, Robert W. to Josephine E. Brinkley 5-31-1869 (6-1-1869) [Ce]
Hooper, T. S. to Emma D. Riggan 12-29-1879 (12-31-1879) [Ce]
Hooper, W. C. to Fanny Nichol 8-15-1871 [Ce]
Hooper, W. J. to E. L. Lovell 12-16-1859 (12-21-1859) [Ce]
Hooper, William to Susan F. Casey 10-23-1861 [Ce]
Hooper, William M. to Dilcy E. Vick 11-26-1866 [Ce]
Hooper, Wm. to Lizzie Minor 11-13-1879 (11-15-1879) B [Ce]
Hooper, Wm. H. to Nora P. Alley 12-13-1873 (12-14-1873) [Ce]
Howe, F. B. to Elizabeth Newsom 12-18-1866 (12-19-1866) [Ce]
Howel, Alfred to Elvira Stringfellow 8-27-1863 [Ce]
Howell, William to Martha Crumpler 7-28-1864 [Ce]
Hows, R. J. to Margret A. Dozier 1-23-1869 (1-27-1869) [Ce]
Hows, S. H. to Nancy Lovell 2-13-1867 (2-14-1867) [Ce]
Huddleston, Andrew to Creecy Pegram 10-16-1867 (10-19-1867) B [Ce]
Huddleston, Berry to Harret Robertson 11-13-1873 (11-14-1873) B [Ce]
Hudgens, A. J. to F. Everette 4-3-1861 (4-7-1861) [Ce]
Hudgens, A. L. to Margret Harris 10-19-1869 (10-23-1869) [Ce]
Hudgens, Ben to Hester Sherron 2-19-1870 (3-6-1870) B [Ce]
Hudgens, Benjamin W. to Martha Shearron 12-3-1868 (12-4-1868) [Ce]
Hudgens, Giddy to Floria Harding 1-15-1880 B [Ce]
Hudgens, J. Z. to Amelia Harris 9-25-1856 [Ce]
Hudgens, Morris to America Hudgens 12-10-1874 (12-13-1874) B [Ce]
Hudgens, T. Hu to Ann E. Shearon 1-14-1867 [Ce]
Hudgens, Wm. Henry to Lucinda Hyde 1-30-1873 (2-2-1873) B [Ce]
Hudgens, York to Josephine Hudgeons 1-6-1870 (1-7-1870) B [Ce]
Hudsan, G. D. to Viola Nichol 2-15-1879 (no return) [Ce]
Huett, Price to Bedy Speight 12-23-1875 (12-22?-1875) B [Ce]
Humbold, William to R. S. Nickens 3-13-1857 (3-17-1857) [Ce]
Humphrey, Alex to Mary J. Hunter 2-5-1874 B [Ce]
Humphreys, Doss to Mary Nicholson 1-1-1875 B [Ce]
Hunt, A. J. to Josie Williams 9-28-1876 (10-1-1876) [Ce]
Hunt, Greene W. to Sarah M. Perdue 1-18-1870 [Ce]
Hunt, Henry to L. Y.? Harris 12-18-1880 (12-23-1880) B [Ce]
Hunt, J. H. W. to Sarah P. Gupton 1-23-1872 [Ce]
Hunt, John K. to Mary Teasley 11-26-1872 [Ce]

Hunt, L. E. to Mary Hudgens 2-21-1862 (3-6-1862) [Ce]
Hunt, Leonidas to L. A. McCormack 4-4-1857 [Ce]
Hunt, Richard to Mary Shaw 1-13-1870 B [Ce]
Hunt, Simon to Lydia Humphreys 9-14-1867 (9-15-1867) B [Ce]
Hunt, William J. to Lassa A. Dowlen 8-14-1860 (8-16-1860) [Ce]
Hunt, Willie W. to Olive W. S. Wilson 3-11-1868 (3-12-1868) [Ce]
Hunt, Wm. C. to Nannie E. Walker 4-15-1876 (4-27-1876) [Ce]
Hunter, Benjamin to Emer Pardue 10-25-1872 (10-26-1872) B [Ce]
Hunter, D. A. to L. E. Morris 12-19-1859 [Ce]
Hunter, Drue to Mahala Beggar 7-13-1881 B [Ce]
Hunter, James to P. A. F. Jones 4-8-1858 (4-9-1858) [Ce]
Hunter, John O. to M. A. Balthrop 8-7-1858 (8-10-1858) [Ce]
Hunter, Samuel to Ella? Teasley 9-10-1870 B [Ce]
Hunter, T. D. to Bettie Sanderlin 12-20-1873 (12-23-1873) [Ce]
Hunter, T. W. to E. J. Murphey 10-27-1857 (10-29-1857) [Ce]
Hunter, W. C. to Sophrona Walker 9-16-1861 (9-17-1861) [Ce]
Hutton, Daniel R. to Betsy Jane Muellins 5-19-1874 (5-20-1874) [Ce]
Hutton, Thomas F. to Martha Newsom 3-18-1865 [Ce]
Hutton, W. C. to Julia A. Pegram 7-1-1862 [Ce]
Hutton, W. C. jr. to I. J. Gallaher 2-2-1872 (2-7-1872) [Ce]
Hutton, Z. T. to M. A. Osborne 4-23-1865 [Ce]
Hyde, J. B. to Beattrice Fry 11-27-1878 (11-28-1878) [Ce]
Hyde, Jesse to A. Walker 8-23-1867 (8-25-1867) B [Ce]
Hyde, Levi to Craleney A. Pennington 8-6-1872 (8-7-1872) B [Ce]
Hyde, Richard to Lieu Bradley 11-18-1879 (11-19-1879) B [Ce]
Hyde, William to Fanny Hudgens 12-27-1866 (12-28-1866) B [Ce]
Inman, R. H. to Martha A. C. Williams 1-17-1868 (1-22-1868) [Ce]
Ivey, James to Alice E. Shubert 4-27-1871 (4-30-1871) [Ce]
Jackson, Burrell to Maggie Brown 3-5-1877 (3-7-1877) [Ce]
Jackson, C. C. to D. A. Jackson 9-18-1867 B [Ce]
Jackson, John T. to Mary T. Pace 12-28-1867 []
Jackson, O. D. to M. E. Shubert 10-30-1858 [Ce]
Jackson, Rufus to Eliza Nicholson 4-27-1867 (4-28-1867) [Ce]
Jackson, William to Ellen A. Hooper 1-13-1869 (1-14-1869) [Ce]
Jackson, Wm. to L. Russell 7-6-1857 (7-9-1857) [Ce]
Jarnnett, W. S. to Minnie S. Ellis 10-25-1878 (10-27-1878) [Ce]
Jennett, Frank to Lucy A. Knox 1-13-1868 (1-16-1868) [Ce]
Jennett, Zack to Henretta Knox 4-15-1873 (4-17-1873) [Ce]
Jo___, Clinton to Emily Major 5-17-1880 (5-18-1880) [Ce]
Johns, Wade M. to Nancy Thompson 3-17-1864 (3-18-1864) [Ce]
Johnson, G. W. to E. A. Chambliss 10-22-1879 (10-23-1879) [Ce]
Johnson, George to Jane Crowder 12-16-1878 B [Ce]
Johnson, J. B. to G. A. Harris 7-3-1876 (7-4-1876) [Ce]
Johnson, Jas. W. to G. A. E. Walker 3-4-1858 (3-7-1858) [Ce]
Johnson, R. J. to Mary J. Harper 5-3-1873 [Ce]
Johnson, W. N. to Louisa Majors 6-11-1870 (6-16-1870) [Ce]
Jones, Alfred to Elizabeth Edgin 12-21-1861 (12-24-1861) [Ce]
Jones, Bailie P. to Emma Farmer 3-28-1874 [Ce]
Jones, Clinton to Emily Major 5-17-1880 (5-18-1880) [Ce]
Jones, Frank to Ellen Stewart 1-1-1874 (1-2-1874) B [Ce]
Jones, Hiram L. to Parthenia Coleman 12-27-1870 (12-29-1870) [Ce]
Jones, Isaac N. to Mariah L. Prescott 7-4-1859 [Ce]
Jones, S. L. to N. L. Hale 12-4-1877 (12-9-1877) [Ce]
Jones, Thos. C. to M. R. Johnson 3-20-1860 [Ce]

Jones, W. R. H. to Martha A. Dill 8-11-1875 (8-12-1875) [Ce]
Jones, Wm. to Mary B. Gupton 12-20-1875 [Ce]
Jones, Zackariah to Harriet Halstead 12-25-1875 (12-26-1875) [Ce]
Jordan, D. M. to Virginia T. Croach 12-26-1861 [Ce]
Jordan, John to Tennessee Bradford 10-9-1873 B [Ce]
Jordon, B. M. to Margia J. Link 2-15-1881 (2-17-1881) [Ce]
Judd, J. H. to S. B. C. Exum 6-19-1869 (6-20-1869) [Ce]
Justice, D. J. to M. C. Perdue 8-3-1858 [Ce]
Justice, J. A. to E. T. Walker 3-17-1868 [Ce]
Justice, Lewis H. to Mary Hudgens 12-27-1879 (12-28-1879) B [Ce]
Justice, R. E. to R. A. Walker 9-4-1875 (9-5-1875) [Ce]
Keith, Isaac to Briley Flenen 8-1-1880 [Ce]
Kelley, James B to Sarah A. Major 8-31-1868 (8?-2-1868) [Ce]
Kellum, George to Emaline Newsom 4-19-1867 (4-20-1867) B [Ce]
Kellum, George to Mary Greer 5-14-1870 (5-21-1870) B [Ce]
Kellum, Lewis to Lizzie Duncen 4-4-1876 (4-7-1876) B [Ce]
Kellum, Shadrick to Susan Hutton 5-11-1870 (5-13-1870) B [Ce]
Kellum, W. W. to G. V. H. Kreider 9-17-1861 (9-19-1861) [Ce]
Kelly, G. W. to Mary T. Frazier 12-14-1867 (12-16-1867) [Ce]
Kenney, Wm. E. to Mary Ceerby 9-12-1873 [Ce]
Kerby, Marshall to Elizabeth Watkins 2-14-1868 B [Ce]
Kidd, Henry N. to Elizabeth Dozier 12-28-1866 B [Ce]
King, John A. to Mattie Allen? 12-24-1870 (12-25-1870) [Ce]
Kirkpatrick, J. M. to M. A. Nye 2-12-1880 [Ce]
Kirkpatrick, Sam to M. R. Hooper 2-12-1867? (2-13-1861) [Ce]
Kirkpatrick, W. B. to P. W. Dismukes 4-15-1873 (4-16-1873) [Ce]
Kline, Walter J. to Mary Ann Hutton 6-18-1872 [Ce]
Knight, A. to Rebeca Wilson 12-2-1867 (12-12-1867) [Ce]
Knight, A. W. to Mollie E. Dozier 9-27-1877 [Ce]
Knight, Geo. to M. A. Chambliss 11-14-1860 (11-16-1860) [Ce]
Knight, James to Sarah Ramer 1-9-1860 (1-13-1860) [Ce]
Knight, John to Julia Adcock 1-29-1877 [Ce]
Knight, John F. to Sally G. Ramer 4-8-1870 (4-10-1870) [Ce]
Knight, Joseph to Mary White 2-8-1878 (2-7?-1878) B [Ce]
Knight, R. B. to Frances Morris 10-6-1870 [Ce]
Knight, W. H. to S. D. A. Barnes 9-25-1880 (9-26-1880) [Ce]
Knight, William to Luvina Anderson 3-25-1874 (3-27-1874) B [Ce]
Knox, M. M. to Allice Haggerd 11-18-1876 (11-19-1876) [Ce]
Knox, R. M. to Sarah E. Vanhook 4-20-1876 (4-26-1876) [Ce]
Krantz, H. P. to Emily L. Walker 12-4-1879 [Ce]
Krantz, Joseph to Matilda Oliver 9-21-1875 (9-23-1875) [Ce]
Krantz, Joseph to Virgina Hooper 7-18-1868 (7-19-1868) [Ce]
Krantz, Mike to Judah A. Newman 1-28-1871 [Ce]
Krantz, Preston to Sarah A. Richardson 10-27-1870 (10-30-1870) [Ce]
Krantz, Thomas to Nannie Rose 12-23-1876 [Ce]
Lane, Frank to Eliza Cheatham 1-3-1868 B [Ce]
Laughlin, Cornelius O. to Bridget Long 2-11-1860 (4-22-1860) [Ce]
Laughlin, Thos. R. to Virginia A. Halstead 1-23-1869 (2-3-1869) [Ce]
Laughran, John N. to Martha E. Harris 9-2-1869 (9-5-1869) [Ce]
Lauson, James to Fannie Nichols 3-31-1871 B [Ce]
Lawrence, W. P. to M. A. Lenox 9-25-1880 (9-26-1880) [Ce]
Lee, E. L. to Jennie Hudgens 11-16-1876 B [Ce]
Lee, John J. to Mary C. Whelus 12-10-1870 (12-11-1870) [Ce]
Lee, Myatt to Clora Willis 1-20-1874 B [Ce]

Lee, R. to A. Binkley 12-23-1856 (12-25-1856) [Ce]
Lee, Wyatt to Lucy Temple 3-20-1869 (3-24-1869) B [Ce]
Leeter, E. D. to M. F. Morris 4-16-1857 [Ce]
Lenox, James J. to Harriett C. Peebles 1-10-1860 [Ce]
Lenox, Joseph to Eliza Hitower 3-20-1869 (3-24-1869) B [Ce]
Lewis, Charles to Mollie Hooper 2-17-1877 (2-27-1877) B [Ce]
Lewis, James D. to Lucy C. Whitfield 5-6-1876 (5-7-1876) [Ce]
Lewis, Lorenzo to Pat Berthrite 4-24-1880 (4-25-1880) B [Ce]
Liles, Elenso D. to Alice E. Herrin 12-4-1875 (12-16-1875) [Ce]
Lipe, Aaron to A. T. Greene 4-12-1871 (4-13-1871) [Ce]
Littrell, William to Ann Chadowin 7-14-1879 (7-17-1879) [Ce]
Lockert, W. S. to Virginia C. Bradley 2-14-1878 [Ce]
Long, S. W. to Alice Highland 4-27-1881 (5-1-1881) [Ce]
Looney, J. A. to Carrie Dowlen 10-4-1869 [Ce]
Lovejoy, W. P. to Anna M. Lowe 11-22-1871 [Ce]
Lovell, A. B. to L. M. Crouch 7-22-1861 (7-25-1861) [Ce]
Lovell, B. P. to Maggie Jane Slump 11-17-1879 (11-19-1879) [Ce]
Lovell, Charles B. to Selina J. Sneed 12-16-1867 (12-19-1867) [Ce]
Lovell, F. P. to E. E. (Mrs.) Curfman 12-14-1871 (12-19-1871) [Ce]
Lovell, G. L. to Bell Hooper 11-17-1877 (11-22-1877) [Ce]
Lovell, J. H. to Harriet Cullum 1-23-1869 (1-27-1869) [Ce]
Lovell, John H. to Laura A. Hooper 1-25-1876 (1-26-1876) [Ce]
Lovell, L. W. jr. to Mary J. Brown 2-28-1877 [Ce]
Lovell, R. G. to S. E. Jordan 10-14-1874 (10-15-1874) [Ce]
Lovell, W. C. to Mary E. Bradford 7-6-1868 [Ce]
Lovell, W. L. to Almier Brown 7-20-1881 [Ce]
Lyles, Joseph to Anna Lee 3-12-1874 B [Ce]
Lyles, William to Lorey Bratton 8-2-1878 (8-4-1878) [Ce]
Lynn, Austin O. to Sallie P. Fulghum 7-11-1864 (7-14-1864) [Ce]
Lyttle, George to Frances Critts 3-12-1868 [Ce]
Maberry, H. M. to Fredonia Hagwewood 2-18-1873 [Ce]
Maberry, J. W. to M. P. Gupton 12-27-1873 (1-1-1874) [Ce]
Maberry, Joseph to Marth A. Ford 2-17-1857 (2-18-1857) [Ce]
Major, G. W. C. C. to Judy A. Jones 9-26-1861 [Ce]
Major, George to Anna Hunt 2-1-1873 B [Ce]
Major, George to Martha Basford 12-18-1869 (12-23-1869) [Ce]
Major, George W. to George Ann Walton 5-2-1872 (5-3-1872) B [Ce]
Major, Joshua B. to Emily T. Chambliss 10-14-1868 (10-15-1868) [Ce]
Major, Rufus to Catie Walton 5-2-1872 (5-3-1872) B [Ce]
Majors, Jas. H. to Mary E. Justice 11-5-1857 [Ce]
Mallory, David to Louisa Head 12-26-1877 (12-27-1877) B [Ce]
Mallory, G. P. to C. H. Newsom 2-7-1876 (2-10-1876) [Ce]
Mallory, Jack to Rosell Williams 12-26-1873 B [Ce]
Mallory, Levi to Marina Williams 12-18-1879 (2-20-1879?) B [Ce]
Mallury, Levi to Mexina Williams 2-18-1879 (2-20-1879) B [Ce]
Maney?, Roger J. to Maggie A. Hamble 12-26-1876 (12-27-1876) [Ce]
Marall, James W. to Sarah Johnson 10-22-1874 [Ce]
Maran, B. H. to Rowena L. Nicholson 11-25-1879 (11-26-1879) [Ce]
Marewell, Jasper to Mary Biggs 12-24-1867 (12-25-1867) [Ce]
Marlow, Tobias to Sarah West 3-25-1874 [Ce]
Martin, J. M. to R. C. Brown 3-2-1867 [Ce]
Martin, William B. to Martha J. Boyte 4-13-1878 (no return) [Ce]
Marwarning, W. L. to T. A. N. Gray 5-29-1858 (5-30-1858) [Ce]
Mathews, A. A. to Alice V. Hooper 11-10-1880 [Ce]

Mathews, Elijah to Martha Sweat 8-13-1878 B [Ce]
Mathews, William H. to Lethy B. Knight 11-26-1868   [Ce]
Matthews, James D. to Mary C. Jones 12-7-1871 (12-14-1871) [Ce]
Maxey, G. W. to Martha Walker 12-22-1880 (12-29-1880) [Ce]
Maxey, James to Josephine A. Walker 10-29-1877   [Ce]
Maxey, Jas. B. to Louvendy F. Teasley 12-21-1878 (12-22-1878) [Ce]
Maxey, W. T. to Zepharin O. M. Hunt 12-28-1869 [Ce]
Maxey, Wilson to Mary E. Wall 11-7-1874 (11-8-1874) [Ce]
Maxwell, Jerry to Elizabeth Abanathy 7-30-1867 (8-1-1867) [Ce]
Mayer, eorge to Melinda Demumbra 12-10-1857 (12-11-1857) [Ce]
Mayes, R. J. to B. B. Fulgham 3-11-1877 [Ce]
Mayfield, William to C. A. Forehand 1-6-1863 (1-8-1863) [Ce]
Mayo, James H. to Ann E. Felts 9-29-1873 (10-1-1873) [Ce]
Mayo, Stephen to Frances Binkley 10-17-1877   [Ce]
Mays, Henry to Julia Knight 5-28-1877 B [Ce]
Mays, J. W. to July Harrington 3-17-1881   [Ce]
Mays, James T. to E. P. Smith 12-6-1860 (12-11-1860) [Ce]
Mays, Joel F. to Mary N. Berry 12-7-1857 (12-10-1857) [Ce]
Mays, John A. to Adar R. Brown 9-24-1872   [Ce]
Mays, John J. to S. P. Carney 6-21-1862   [Ce]
Mays, Joseph to Penina Pegram 8-24-1870 (8-28-1870) [Ce]
Mays, Joseph F. to Molly A. Charlton 1-19-1877 (1-23-1877)   [Ce]
Mays, Newsom B. to Elenor Kellum 11-24-1858   [Ce]
Mays, Thomas to Susan Ussery 1-9-1873 B [Ce]
Mays, Thomas to Susan Ussey 1-11-1873 B [Ce]
Mays, Wm. P. to Rebecca J. Dunn 10-1-1860 (10-10-1860) [Ce]
Mays?, J. H. to Mary E. Butts 11-8-1876 (11-23-1876) [Ce]
McCall, C. C. to Mary E. Dozier 8-14-1878 (8-15-1878) [Ce]
McCommack, Thomas to Nancy A. Binkley 7-19-1859 (7-21-1859) [Ce]
McCormack, N. to Sarah King 4-27-1861 (4-28-1861) [Ce]
McCormack, Robert to Mary Nicholsen 10-12-1876   [Ce]
McCormack, Robt. to Mary Ann Logan 11-25-1876 (11-26-1876) [Ce]
McCormic, James to Faney Johns 6-22-1866 (6-25-1866) [Ce]
McCrea, Moses to Mattie Hale 1-22-1876 B [Ce]
McCree, Moses to Lucinda Bush 3-18-1869 B [Ce]
McDaniel, W. T. to Mary Baker 6-30-1879 (7-1-1879) [Ce]
McFarlin, Edward B. to Mary E. Sutton 5-5-1858 (5-6-1858) [Ce]
McGhee, J. S. to Savanah T. Gray 10-29-1872 (11-10-1872) [Ce]
McGhee, William F. to Elizabeth A. Murff 7-27-1869 (7-28-1869) [Ce]
McNeal, Wm. Murry to America McNeal 10-20-1874   [Ce]
McQuary?, G. W. to Jane Dozier 4-10-1866 (4-11-1866) [Ce]
McRussell, William to Martha Jane Perkins 4-5-1871 (4-6-1871) [Ce]
Medows, J. C. to Annie A. Riggan 12-10-1874 (12-15-1874) [Ce]
Menroe, Jackson to Amy Hagewood 12-15-1876 (12-21-1876) [Ce]
Meriham, L. G. to M. C. Porch 2-5-1868 (2-7-1868) [Ce]
Merril, Mack to Nancy Washington 3-23-1871 B [Ce]
Miles, B. S. to Amanda Hooper 12-10-1856 (12-11-1856) [Ce]
Miles, H. C. to A. A. Clark 6-28-1861 (6-20-1861) [Ce]
Miles, H. W. to Permelia Stewart 4-12-1869 (4-13-1869) [Ce]
Miles, W. H. to Aquilla Perdue 1-23-1867 (1-24-1867) [Ce]
Miles, W. H. to Moaning? Jones 1-13-1877 (1-18-1877) [Ce]
Miller, W. T. to A. Brinkley 1-2-1858 (1-3-1858) [Ce]
Miller, William J. to Susan H. Mackbee 12-19-1860 (12-20-1860) [Ce]
Miner?, F. to E. Patterson 12-26-1876 B [Ce]

Mitchel, Phillip H. to Emily Crider 2-1-1879 (2-5-1879) [Ce]
Montgomery, John to George Ann Harris 12-16-1878 B [Ce]
Moore, M. L. to Virginia A. Fulghum 7-11-1864 (7-14-1864) [Ce]
Moore, R. to E. A. Alley 8-25-1859 [Ce]
Moore, William to E. Bell Williams 1-26-1872 (1-13?-1872) [Ce]
Moorman, J. B. to Lula (Miss) Warren 9-3-1878 (9-4-1878) [Ce]
Moran, J. P. to Nancy M. Stewart 2-5-1858 [Ce]
Morison, W. W. to Mary J. Hamlet 6-9-1858 [Ce]
Morris, B. C. to N. N. Miles 2-6-1861 (2-8-1861) [Ce]
Morris, H. L. to Nancy Ann Binkley 10-2-1869 (10-3-1869) [Ce]
Morris, J. to H. A. Page 1-24-1880 (1-25-1880) [Ce]
Morris, James W. to Eliza Durard 10-20-1866 (10-21-1866) [Ce]
Morris, Joseph to Martha W. Gibbs 1-30-1868 [Ce]
Morris, Joshua W. to Angeline Binkley 12-27-1876 (12-28-1876) [Ce]
Morris, Joshuwa to Melvina A. Morris 4-12-1862 [Ce]
Morris, Nathan to Mary A. Henderson 1-23-1862 [Ce]
Morris, Simion to Fannie Gibbs 3-5-1878 (3-6-1878) [Ce]
Morris, W. H. to Martha P. Felts 2-15-1860 (2-16-1860) [Ce]
Morris, W. L. to C. M. Lewis 7-26-1858 (8-1-1858) [Ce]
Morris, W. L. to Eliza Ann Keeler 10-23-1869 (10-24-1869) [Ce]
Morris, W. W. to M. A. Brunrack? 2-18-1879 (2-23-1879) [Ce]
Moses, William D. to Allice C. Williams 1-7-1871 (1-8-1871) [Ce]
Mosier, J. K. P. to Martha Darrow 8-10-1865 [Ce]
Mosier, J. P. to Nancy M. Hampton 11-27-1873 [Ce]
Mosier, Joseph to Mary Knight 11-1-1858 (11-3-1858) [Ce]
Mosley, John F. to D. A. Nicholson 2-14-1860 (2-16-1860) [Ce]
Mosley, Peter to Susan Jackson 3-20-1869 (3-21-1869) B [Ce]
Mosley, Robert D. to Eliz. Majors 8-13-1859 (9-4-1859) [Ce]
Mullins, G. W. to Catharine M. Denny 8-6-1866 (8-7-1866) [Ce]
Mumpford, George to Polly Jordan 4-3-1869 (4-6-1869) B [Ce]
Murff, Geo. F. to Ellata Carney 5-14-1878 (5-16-1878) [Ce]
Murphey, Robert to Sarah Ann Jane Akin 5-27-1871 (5-29-1871) [Ce]
Murphy, C. W. to P. W. Council 11-1-1869 [Ce]
Nabors, B. H. to T. M. Binkley 8-17-1861 [Ce]
Nabors, Isaac W. to Elizabeth Vick 10-25-1858 [Ce]
Nanney, John M. to Ann E. Clifton 1-3-1870 (1-9-1870) [Ce]
Nanney, William to Sarah F. Walls 5-22-1878 [Ce]
Neal, W. C. to E. H. Brown 1-4-1879 (1-5-1879) [Ce]
Neblett, W. L. to M. J. Randolph 1-14-1857 (1-20-1857) [Ce]
Neighbors, Bynam G. to Ellen Boyd 10-14-1871 (10-15-1871) [Ce]
Neighbors, G. W. to Anne Kistley 7-28-1880 (7-29-1880) [Ce]
Neighbors, William to Milly Demumbra 6-8-1874 [Ce]
Newlen, Thos. A. to Susan Binkley 7-15-1864 [Ce]
Newman, John T. to Mary Jane Dowlen 10-29-1870 (10-30-1870) [Ce]
Newman, M. C. to Everlin Krantz 2-23-1881 (2-24-1881) [Ce]
Newsom, A. J. to E. K. Lovell 1-3-1866 (1-4-1866) [Ce]
Newsom, Davy to Catharine Johnson 8-24-1875 B [Ce]
Newsom, Frank to Margaret Robertson 1-25-1873 B [Ce]
Newsom, Leonedus to Judah A. Dozier 12-5-1870 (12-7-1870) [Ce]
Newsom, Newton to Clarice? Shelton 4-24-1880 (4-25-1880) B [Ce]
Newsom, Solomon to Lucy Shelton 2-2-1874 (2-14-1874) B [Ce]
Newton, S. W. to Susan McFall 10-29-1874 [Ce]
Nichol, Lewey to Metilda Hunter 4-26-1867 (4-27-1867) B [Ce]
Nichol, W. C. C. to Thursa C. Hooper 12-18-1861 (12-22-1861) [Ce]

Nichol, Robert L. to Una Hooper 8-15-1864   [Ce]
Nichols, David W. to Nancy C. Cullum 6-4-1870 (6-5-1870) [Ce]
Nichols, James to Frances Felts 6-26-1869 (6-27-1869) [Ce]
Nichols, Richard to Mary Humphreys 5-10-1872 (5-11-1872) B [Ce]
Nichols, William B. to Nancy T. Hooper 1-10-1857   [Ce]
Nicholson, B. to N. C. Walker 5-10-1871 (5-11-1871) [Ce]
Nicholson, Colemon to Victoria Hunt 12-28-1872 (12-29-1872) [Ce]
Nicholson, D. B. to A. T. Nicholson 10-24-1876 (10-25-1876) [Ce]
Nicholson, G. B. to Mary A. E. Majors 9-21-1859 (9-23-1859) [Ce]
Nicholson, Griffin to Emma Doyd? 7-3-1880 (7-4-1880) [Ce]
Nicholson, H. G. to M. M. Boyd 2-3-1877 (2-5-1877) [Ce]
Nicholson, J. B. to Martha Shearon 11-26-1879 (11-30-1879) [Ce]
Nicholson, J. J. to Elizabeth W. Harris 2-2-1869   [Ce]
Nicholson, J. T. to Martha F. Durham 9-2-1871 (9-5-1871) [Ce]
Nicholson, Jesse to Anacha? Teasley 5-21-1873 B [Ce]
Nicholson, Joseph to Amanda Hyde 9-4-1880 (9-5-1880) B [Ce]
Nicholson, M. to Eliz. Cain 12-27-1856   [Ce]
Nicholson, Montgomery to Rebecca McDaniel 1-5-1871   [Ce]
Nicholson, N. T. to R. B. Chambliss 9-26-1876 (9-27-1876) [Ce]
Nicholson, R. F. to Mary E. Hunt 12-25-1878   [Ce]
Nicholson, Ruffin to Emaline Batson 3-2-1872 (3-7-1872) B [Ce]
Nicholson, S. A. to Nancy Pace 11-18-1875   [Ce]
Nicholson, Scott to Mary A. Murphey 5-12-1871   [Ce]
Nicholson, W. P. to Emily Frazier 10-25-1879 (10-26-1879) [Ce]
Nickolson, G. B. to E. N. Nickolson 1-8-1868 (1-9-1868) [Ce]
Nighs?, John F. to Elizabeth Ranor 11-22-1878   [Ce]
Noe, E. A. to M. E. Boyd 12-17-1877 (12-18-1877) [Ce]
Nolen, Edward M. to Laura Dye 2-4-1861 (2-18-1861) [Ce]
Nunley, John to Nancy Sittner? 5-25-1868 (5-26-1868) [Ce]
Nye, D. N. to Lou Ingle 1-7-1874 (1-15-1874) [Ce]
Oakley, C. A. to Frances E. Abanathey 1-16-1875 (1-18-1875) [Ce]
Obearr, John to Sarah Betis 3-17-1864   [Ce]
Obrian, Wm. H. to Margret J. Gibbs 10-4-1869 (10-5-1869) [Ce]
Obrien, Robert S. to Mary E. G. Hooper 11-29-1871   [Ce]
Oliver, Wm. to Elizabeth Farmer 12-25-1871   [Ce]
Oliver, Wm. H. to Jane Parrish 7-13-1869   [Ce]
Osborn, J. M. to Sarah C. Miles 1-28-1874   [Ce]
Osborn, Wm. F. to Lue F. Dillingham 2-14-1877   [Ce]
Osborne, John B. to Nancy I. Dozier 3-16-1867 (3-17-1867) [Ce]
Osborne, John B. to Nancy J. Dozier 3-10-1867   [Ce]
Osborne, Thos. T. to E. B. Henderson 1-9-1858   [Ce]
Osburn, James N. to Sarah C. Brinkley 4-5-1859 (4-4?-1859) [Ce]
Outlaw?, J. H. to Q. R. Bobbitt 5-8-880 (5-9-1880) [Ce]
Owen, Jessie L. to Elmina Morriss 10-15-1874   [Ce]
Owen, Thos. A. to Jane E. Fox 12-13-1869 (12-16-1869) [Ce]
Owen, Wm. H. to Musedore McClure 7-25-1866   [Ce]
Owen, Z. W. to Annie M. McDaniel 10-24-1879 (10-26-1879) [Ce]
Owen, Z. W. to Sarah A. Jennett 11-18-1872 (11-19-1872) [Ce]
Owens, T. R. to Chyntha? Nickolson 1-27-1868   [Ce]
Owens, T. R. to Cyntha A. Nicholson 1-28-1868   [Ce]
Pace, John R. to Mary J. Bigger 1-16-1867 (1-17-1867) [Ce]
Pace, T. J. to M. A. Teasley 1-6-1879 (1-8-1879) [Ce]
Pace, W. H. to Martha Walker 12-9-1874 (12-10-1874) [Ce]
Pace, W. I. to Mahal Walker 1-16-1860 (1-19-1860) [Ce]

Pack, B. L. to Mattie E. Dillingham 2-6-1879 (2-20-1879) [Ce]
Pack, E. W. to M. E. Curfman 12-22-1875 (12-26-1875) [Ce]
Pack, George to Sarah Paterson 11-1-1872 (10?-3-1872) B [Ce]
Pack, Isham to Susan Ussery 1-3-1876 B [Ce]
Pack, J. L. to C. C. Smith 3-17-1863 [Ce]
Pack, L. J. to Letitia Dillingham 5-4-1864 [Ce]
Pack, L. L. to M. E. Smith 3-5-1877 (3-7-1877) [Ce]
Pack, M. V. to S. P. Garland 1-27-1877 (1-28-1877) [Ce]
Pack, R. M. to Mary Ann Sweney 6-2-1863 [Ce]
Pack, Wm. H. to Samuella McTulere? 2-11-1873 (2-13-1873) [Ce]
Page, Absalum to Mary Turner 12-29-1859 [Ce]
Page, Havy to Susan E. Douglas 11-28-1866 [Ce]
Page, M. to P. Weaklkey 12-24-1857 [Ce]
Page, William to Maggie Ballard 1-21-1880 (1-22-1880) [Ce]
Page, Woody to Mahala Wilson 2-7-1880 (2-10-1880) [Ce]
Pakins, C. C. to Sarah J. Cross 4-17-1857 (4-21-1857) [Ce]
Pane, John to Mehala Hooper 9-24-1856 (9-25-1856) [Ce]
Paradise, Isaac E. to Eliza Tate 3-13-1877 [Ce]
Parkerson, Frank to Spatia Sherron 12-18-1874 B [Ce]
Parkerson, Henry to Mollie Hays? 4-8-1876 B [Ce]
Parthene, Robt. to Elizabeth Boyt 10-27-1869 (10-28-1869) [Ce]
Paschal, Benja. to Louisa Moore 1-4-1860 (1-6-1860) [Ce]
Patrick, C. H. to Bettie Smith 6-8-1881 (6-10-1881) [Ce]
Patterson, Luke to Margret Shearon 6-14-1879 B [Ce]
Patterson, Marion to Rachael Washington 12-7-1878 (12-12-1878) B [Ce]
Patton, John to George Ann Fults 12-22-1877 (12-23-1877) [Ce]
Payne, Green Wood to Sallie W. Fulghum 6-3-1869 [Ce]
Pegram, James to L. A. Gallaher 9-5-1868 [Ce]
Pegram, John to Ellic Barclift 5-31-1870 (6-19-1870) B [Ce]
Pegram, R. W. to M. E. Fulghum 9-17-1861 (9-25-1861) [Ce]
Pegram, Roger to Julia Williams 10-26-1863 (10-28-1863) [Ce]
Pegram, Sill to Thena Carter 4-3-1872 (4-7-1872) B [Ce]
Pegram, William J. to Deborah E. Porch 2-4-1865 (2-5-1868) [Ce]
Pegram, William M. to Ellen D. Gallaher 2-20-1864 [Ce]
Pennington, Robt. to Susan Elliott 12-31-1861 [Ce]
Pentecast, W. H. to E. M. Pentecast 1-4-1859 [Ce]
Pentecost, J. T. to Emeline Sample 10-31-1868 (11-17-1868) [Ce]
Perdue, A. J. to Mary Fetts 8-30-1859 [Ce]
Perdue, A. J. to Mary T. Dowlen 1-11-1872 [Ce]
Perdue, C. J. to Thursey R. Allen 10-28-1873 (10-30-1873) [Ce]
Perdue, D. C. to Penelope Major 8-19-1867 (8-20-1867) [Ce]
Perdue, James M. to Sarah E. Richardson 5-31-1877 (6-31?-1877) [Ce]
Perdue, John to Julia M. Cain 10-21-1858 [Ce]
Perdue, Mason to Mary Evans 12-25-1871 (12-28-1871) B [Ce]
Perdue, T. B. to P. G. Nicholson 11-29-1866 [Ce]
Perdue, Thomas B. to Jane Stewart 12-28-1868 (12-29-1868) [Ce]
Perdue, W. C. to Mary E. Smith 12-28-1859 [Ce]
Perry, Fate to Lucy Mitchel 12-20-1878 (12-21-1878) [Ce]
Perry, George W. to D. P. Olliver 7-13-1872 (7-14-1872) [Ce]
Perry, J. H. to Emily Bailey 12-29-1857 (12-30-1857) [Ce]
Perry, James to Mollie Anderson 4-1-1880 [Ce]
Perry, Lewis to Mary Vess 6-24-1874 (6-26-1874) [Ce]
Perry, Lewis to Texas Walden 10-1-1873 [Ce]
Perry, Littleton to Cyntha Moore 8-11-1857 [Ce]

Perry, M. to Julia A. Moore 10-18-1866 (10-19-1866) [Ce]
Perry, R. T. to Rachel Williams 9-26-1866 [Ce]
Perry, Sampson to Jane Harrenton 11-29-1871 (11-30-1871) [Ce]
Perry, Thos. H. to Lucian Hudgens 1-10-1876 (1-12-1876) [Ce]
Perry, W. T. to Alice C. Carson 4-12-1866 [Ce]
Petway, A. M. to Nannie Williams 7-24-1880 [Ce]
Phillips, Joseph M. to Malinda Swan 6-5-1875 [Ce]
Phipps, N. B. to Eliza F. Hatcher 12-12-1860 (12-17-1860) [Ce]
Pickering, G. S. to H. A. Adkins 1-31-1858 [Ce]
Pickering, G. S. to H. A. Adkins no date (with May 1858) [Ce]
Pinson, G. W. to S. V. Eatherly 2-12-1870 (2-17-1870) [Ce]
Plasters, W. H. to G. F. Teasley 1-11-1860 (1-12-1860) [Ce]
Plasters, W. H. to Sarah Harris 1-8-1868 (1-9-1868) [Ce]
Pool, Frank to Tennessee Miles 12-28-1859 (12-26?-1859) [Ce]
Pool, H. R. to M. R. Naney 6-17-1858 [Ce]
Pool, Jas. W. to M. Sanders 8-13-1857 [Ce]
Pool, John A. to George Ann T. Pool 11-11-1868 (11-12-1868) [Ce]
Pool, John A. to P. Comperry 6-14-1859 [Ce]
Pool, W. H. to Jeridine Teasley 11-30-1872 (12-1-1872) [Ce]
Pool, Wm. R. to C. Humphreys 12-24-1857 [Ce]
Powel, Jack to Eliza Shaw 12-26-1878 B [Ce]
Powell, W. H. to Sarah Binkley 9-18-1872 (9-19-1872) [Ce]
Power, Jno. L. W. to D. M. Brinkley 1-6-1881 [Ce]
Powers, John to Marina Walker 7-15-1875 B [Ce]
Praw?, John to Mary Ann Hall 3-9-1868 (3-10-1868) [Ce]
Price, D. L. to Josephine Nannie 3-6-1868 (3-8-1868) [Ce]
Price, L. D. to Sarah E. Walls 1-24-1866 [Ce]
Price, R. W. to Sarah S. Jordan 1-2-1875 (1-3-1875) [Ce]
Price, William to Martha Purnell 2-16-1864 [Ce]
Procter, J. M. to Dora Hagewood 10-9-1876 (10-13-1876) [Ce]
Procter, John R. to Martha Felts 1-4-1871 [Ce]
Proctor, F. M. to Sarah A. Simpkins 3-12-1866 [Ce]
Puckett, Henry W. to Melissa Randle 7-4-1878 (no return) [Ce]
Puckett, T. J. to Mary Morris 12-20-1864 [Ce]
Ragan, A. C. to Lutitia Dozier 1-1-1873 [Ce]
Ragan, Henry H. to Celestea P. Slump 10-14-1873 (10-13?-1873) [Ce]
Ramer, Cheatham to Tennessee Knight 4-22-1880 [Ce]
Ramer, Edward to Julia Chambliss 12-2-1880 [Ce]
Ramer, Eli M. to Dicy E. Ramer 12-2-1869 [Ce]
Ramer, Geo. W. to F. Y. P. Woodward 6-1-1857 (6-11-1857) [Ce]
Ramer, William R. to Mary D. Felts 10-11-1865 [Ce]
Ransdale, W. B. to E. A. Jennett 12-4-1858 [Ce]
Rasberry, sGeo. W. to Emily Swar 4-18-1859 (4-19-1859) [Ce]
Rase, William to Martha Ann Farmer 8-13-1879 (8-14-1879) [Ce]
Raymer, John M. to Milberry Raymer 1-26-1878 (1-27-1878) [Ce]
Read, B. F. to Mary A. Krantz 5-6-1868 (5-7-1868) [Ce]
Read, G. W. to Sarah F. Sanders 12-24-1870 (12-28-1870) [Ce]
Read, Isaac W. to Sarah J. Cothen 11-12-1863 (11-18-1863) [Ce]
Read, James H. to Lucy Eastridge 10-2-1869 (10-3-1869) [Ce]
Read, Masha C. to Sallie McCall 11-16-1870 (11-17-1870) [Ce]
Read, W. J. to Sarah E. Harris 7-22-1876 [Ce]
Read, W. W. to E. C. Hudgens 10-27-1860 (11-18-1860) [Ce]
Redd, William P. to Adaline F. Clark 2-13-1863 [Ce]
Redding, James to Tama Yeatman 8-25-1877 (8-26-1877) B [Ce]

Reding, Richard to Tennessee Bennett 3-13-1867 (3-19-1867) [Ce]
Redman, Alexa to Marinda Morris 10-20-1877 (10-21-1877) B [Ce]
Reed, D. A. to Mary M. Harris 4-18-1879 (4-20-1879) [Ce]
Reed, Enoch to Mary Jane Gray 3-15-1881 [Ce]
Reed, James H. to Ivory? G. Stack 8-26-1874 (8-31-1874) [Ce]
Reeves, R. A. to S. A. W. Wright 9-11-1876 (9-14-1876) [Ce]
Reggan, W. J. to A. P. Hooper 11-29-1878 (12-1-1878) [Ce]
Reman, William to Delila Miller 2-24-1874 (2-26-1874) [Ce]
Rhea, L. A. to Mary E. Hale 9-9-1876 (9-10-1876) [Ce]
Richardson, B. C. to Tilda J. Krantz 5-13-1870 [Ce]
Richardson, C. J. to Elizabeth E. Hall 3-26-1864 (3-27-1864) [Ce]
Richardson, John L. to Pracilla Edgin 10-17-1867 [Ce]
Ridge, Jasper to Martha J. Moore 3-23-1864 [Ce]
Riggan, Wm. to Mollie J. Moore 2-8-1881 (2-10-1881) [Ce]
Rinehart, A. J. to Eliza J. Benton 9-19-1876 (9-21-1876) [Ce]
Roach, W. C. to Sarah J. Keeler 9-14-1871 (9-17-1871) [Ce]
Roberts, Clay to Mary J. Anderson 8-12-1875 [Ce]
Robertson, Andrew to Delila Jackson 9-6-1872 (9-7-1872) B [Ce]
Robertson, Andrew to Tennessee Harris 12-24-1866 (12-26-1866) B [Ce]
Robertson, Len to Pauline Anderson 9-18-1880 B [Ce]
Robertson, Wm. L. to J. P. Denny 1-28-1858 [Ce]
Roop?, W. S. to Lucy Millikin 7-9-1879 (7-10-1879) [Ce]
Rooper, Smith to E. J. Turntine 7-16-1867 (SB 1857?) [Ce]
Rose, J. C. B. to Harriet Binkley 5-26-1866 (5-31-1866) [Ce]
Rose, James A. to Martha F. Krantz 12-2-1876 [Ce]
Ross, Olliver to Martha Jones 10-24-1873 B [Ce]
Rossen, J. D. to Mary Jane Knox 4-22-1876 (4-27-1876) [Ce]
Rosson, J. L. to Josaphine Huggins 1-22-1879 (1-23-1879) [Ce]
Rowson, George T. to Lucy Williams 12-26-1868 (12-27-1868) [Ce]
Rudeker, Wm. to Mary Binkley 10-9-1857 [Ce]
Rudolph, George to Elizabeth Hunter 3-30-1880 (3-31-1880) [Ce]
Rudolph, J. R. to J. G. Nicholson 12-16-1857 (12-17-1857) [Ce]
Russell, James L. to Mary Hooper 1-17-1866 [Ce]
Russell, T. W. to Martha Vick 7-27-1863 [Ce]
Russell, William to Frances Rack 5-12-1860 [Ce]
Russell, William to Tennessee Kinchlow? 7-23-1874 [Ce]
Rye, Thomas H. to Martha E. Haywood 5-2-1859 [Ce]
Sample, A. W. to Rose Ann Krantz 7-3-1868 (7-5-1868) [Ce]
Samples, James L. to Sarah Anderson 9-26-1868 (10-1-1868) [Ce]
Samples, W. C. to Parelee Boyte 8-28-1874 [Ce]
Sanders, A. J. to Martha Perry 1-27-1858 [Ce]
Sanders, A. W. to Josephine McCormack 10-21-1875 (10-22-1875) [Ce]
Sanders, H. W. to M. E. Eatherly 12-23-1857 (12-24-1857) [Ce]
Sanders, Isaac W. to Cornela Martin 2-2-1872 (2-4-1872) [Ce]
Sanders, J. W. to M. J. Krantz 3-31-1870 [Ce]
Sanders, J. W. to Rebecca Smith 7-7-1876 (7-16-1876) [Ce]
Sanders, John W. to Martha J. Simmons 2-21-1874 (2-22-1874) [Ce]
Sanders, Jos. E. to Cornelia Boyte 2-26-1881 (2-27-1881) [Ce]
Sanders, M. H. to Lucinda Teasly 8-15-1877 (8-16-1877) [Ce]
Sanders, W. T. to M. A. E. Binkley 9-11-1864 [Ce]
Sanders, W. W. to Mary O'Brien 3-8-1875 (3-9-1875) [Ce]
Satterfield, Hosa to Elizabeth Harris 9-14-1868 (9-15-1868) [Ce]
Satterfield, Mathew to Eliz. Thenabee? 2-24-1857 (5-31-1857) [Ce]
Sayer, Anderson to Milla Jane Wilson 11-16-1867 (12-4-1867) B [Ce]

Sayer, Rubin to Martha Bell 3-2-1878 (3-3-1878) B [Ce]
Sayers, Ruben to Patsey Bell 11-24-1877 B [Ce]
Scott, G. A. to Pheby J. F. Cooper 1-20-1881   [Ce]
Scott, G. A. to Phoebe J. Hooper 1-20-1881   [Ce]
Scott, James to Caroline Hazan 7-28-1870 (7-30-1870) B [Ce]
Scott, Robt. T. to M. E. Wynn 10-6-1869 (10-7-1869) [Ce]
Scott, St. Leger to Alvy J. Greene 1-19-1871   [Ce]
Scott, W. H. to Mary E. Wynn 9-24-1866 (9-25-1866) [Ce]
Scott, W. W. to Ivone H. Woodson 5-28-18878 (5-29-1878) [Ce]
Scruggs, Wm. to Sarah Clinard 10-16-1876 (10-18-1876) [Ce]
Sears, E. G. to Isabella Kellum 5-30-1870 (6-1-1870) [Ce]
Sells, Samuel to Phereby Benefield 3-26-1867 (3-28-1867) [Ce]
Shadowen, Charles R. to Josephine Clark 7-21-1879   [Ce]
Shadrick, James P. to Elizabeth Gillam 3-17-1868   [Ce]
Shadrick, Martin to Susan Sanders 7-12-1871   [Ce]
Sham, J. D. to M. E. Dillingham 5-29-1871   [Ce]
Shaver, Geo. W. to Margret A. Jackson 12-13-1869   [Ce]
Shaw, Aleck to Ann Majors 12-27-1869 (12-28-1869) B [Ce]
Shaw, Guss to Charity Spates 6-8-1872 (6-9-1872) B [Ce]
Shaw, Henry J. to N. W. Shearon 4-11-1859 (4-12-1859) [Ce]
Shaw, J. T. to Bettie Shearen 12-23-1876 (12-24-1876) [Ce]
Shaw, James T. to Mary A. Teasly 12-17-1867 (12-19-1867) [Ce]
Shaw, T. J. to R. T. Murff 12-2-1871 (12-3-1871) [Ce]
Shearin, Claiborne to Ann Shaw 11-24-1866 (11-26-1866) B [Ce]
Shearon, B. F. to Nancy A. Whitworth 8-4-1877 (8-9-1877) [Ce]
Shearon, G. W. to C. J. Vanhook 11-18-1880   [Ce]
Shearon, J. C. to Mary Teasley 11-22-1877   [Ce]
Shearon, J. N. to Mary Jenkins 1-5-1874   [Ce]
Shearon, Jessee to Sarah Harper 12-16-1862   [Ce]
Shearon, W. J. to Nannie E. Newlin 10-27-1877 (10-28-1877) [Ce]
Shearon, W. S. to E. G. Walker 12-15-1877 (12-20-18877) [Ce]
Shearon, Z. to E. W. Flintoff 10-6-1863 (10-7-1863) [Ce]
Shearon, Z. to M. E. Frazier 10-16-1876 (10-19-1876) [Ce]
Shearon, Z. F. to Nancy Harris 9-1-1865   [Ce]
Shearron, P. C. to Elizabeth L. Reece 1-1-1868   [Ce]
Shelton, John to Meriah Ferebee 2-28-1871 B [Ce]
Sheppard, James to Susan Smith 3-14-1872 B [Ce]
Sherron, George to Unis Williams 10-3-1870 (10-16-1870) B [Ce]
Shevers, Ralph to Mary L. Simpson 4-30-1872 (5-5-1872) [Ce]
Shivers, C. J. C. to Martha Demumbra 5-27-1876 (5-28-1876) [Ce]
Shivers, John to Eliz. H. Fetts 2-11-1857   [Ce]
Shivers, W. J. to Nancy E. Nichols 6-3-1872 (6-16-1872) [Ce]
Shooks, Ander to Alice Works 7-21-1881 B [Ce]
Shores, A. T. to Elizabeth H. Perdue 2-25-1861   [Ce]
Simmons, A. J. to Tennessee Eatherly no date (with Feb 1867) [Ce]
Simmons, E. to S. Lewis 6-21-1858 (7-4-1858) [Ce]
Simmons, G. W. to Sarah A. Patton 11-8-1865   [Ce]
Simmons, Henry to Kate Sullivan 7-27-1870 (8-31-1870) [Ce]
Simmons, I. W. to E. J. Hollis 11-4-1875   [Ce]
Simmons, J. H. to N. G. Hudgens 9-26-1878 (9-29-1878) [Ce]
Simmons, James to Martha Perry 11-20-1875 (11-21-1875) [Ce]
Simmons, James S.? to Martha A. Miles 1-12-1881 (1-13-1881) [Ce]
Simmons, Jasper to Nancy D. Sanders 3-1-1863 (3-3-1863) [Ce]
Simmons, Levi to Narcissy Casey 12-29-1857   [Ce]

Simmons, Wm. to E. J. Swaggart 4-11-1859 (4-14-1859) [Ce]
Simpkins, J. G. to Martha J. Simpkins 4-12-1877 [Ce]
Simpkins, J. L. to Julia A. Biggs 2-4-1874 (2-6-1874) [Ce]
Simpkins, J. W. to Lizzie M. Gleaves 4-25-1876 [Ce]
Simpkins, J. W. to T. C. Douglass 7-10-1881 [Ce]
Simpkins, James I. to Susan F. Boyd 9-25-1875 (9-26-1875) [Ce]
Simpkins, John W. to Sarah J. Demumbra 12-27-1869 (12-28-1869) [Ce]
Sisler, Thos. to Elizabeth Smith 10-21-1880 (10-24-1880) [Ce]
Slack, G. D. to Fredonia Whitworth 3-8-1879 (3-13-1879) [Ce]
Sllump, F. H. to Martha E. Dozier 9-7-1859 (9-8-1859) [Ce]
Sloan, Arther A. to Mollie J. Carney 12-21-1880 (12-22-1880) [Ce]
Sloan, George L. to Louisa H. Dow 7-27-1858 (7-29-1858) [Ce]
Sloan, R. B. to M. C. Sloan 9-18-1857 [Ce]
Slodge, Richard to Mariah Hale 10-11-1873 (10-12-1873) B [Ce]
Smith, A. D. to Sarah Harris 10-5-1874 (10-8-1874) [Ce]
Smith, Albert to Adaline T. Miles 4-2-1862 (4-3-1862) [Ce]
Smith, B. F. to Lucy J. Hatcher 1-18-1859 (1-19-1859) [Ce]
Smith, E. W. to Sarah J. Boyle 12-29-1880 (12-30-1880) [Ce]
Smith, Elick to Katie Pardue 12-25-1873 (12-27-1873) B [Ce]
Smith, Elisha to E. C. McCormack 11-12-1860 (11-15-1860) [Ce]
Smith, G. M. to Elizabeth Hunt 10-14-1878 (10-15-1878) [Ce]
Smith, G. W. to Emer L. Hunter 3-4-1878 (3-6-1878) [Ce]
Smith, J. D. to Susannah Maxey 12-4-1871 (12-8-1871) [Ce]
Smith, J. F. to Narcissa O. Harper 2-18-1873 (2-23-1873) [Ce]
Smith, J. O. to Martha P. Hunter 2-23-1875 (2-25-1875) [Ce]
Smith, James to Addie Shearon 12-23-1880 [Ce]
Smith, James M. to Nancy A. T. Edwards 11-8-1876 (11-10-1876) [Ce]
Smith, James W. to Mary Miles 11-4-1862 [Ce]
Smith, John J. to Martha J. Ozburn 2-3-1879 (2-13-1879) [Ce]
Smith, John M. to Mary A. Gupton 4-15-1859 [Ce]
Smith, Joran to Eliza Shaw 5-24-1872 B [Ce]
Smith, Jordan to Nannie Perdue 12-29-1866 B [Ce]
Smith, L. F. to Eliza Gupton 2-4-1878 (2-6-1878) [Ce]
Smith, S. B. to Addie J. Stewart 5-20-1874 [Ce]
Smith, W. S. to Mary E. Neal 12-6-1866 [Ce]
Smith, W. W. to Nancy M. Bobbitt 12-30-1871 (1-4-1872) [Ce]
Smith, Walker to Caity Shelton 4-18-1874 (4-19-1874) B [Ce]
Sneed, N. P. to H. R. Fulgham 1-14-1867 (1-15-1867) [Ce]
Snell, A. E. to E. J. Woodall 4-14-1862 [Ce]
Speight, James to Callinhite? Hyde 3-15-1879 (3-16-1879) B [Ce]
Speight, James to S. A. Greene 2-27-1867 [Ce]
Spencer, Miles D. to Eugenia Herrin 6-2-1877 (6-3-1877) [Ce]
Stack, B. J. to Louisa Miles 12-23-1859 [Ce]
Stack, Benja. J. to Marth J. Alley 4-11-1857 [Ce]
Stack, D. W. to Sallie S. Allen 12-23-1879 [Ce]
Stack, George W. to Tona G. Douglass 12-26-1872 [Ce]
Stack, J. W. to Medora Weakley 8-12-1865 [Ce]
Stack, John R.? to Calvina T. Willson 2-25-1868 (2-27-1868) [Ce]
Stalcup, A. to Sarah J. Cate? 12-30-1867 [Ce]
Stalzey, Henry to Levina E. Smith 11-14-1859 [Ce]
Starns, C. W. to Elvira Walker 7-18-1857 (7-19-1857) [Ce]
Sterry, C. W. to M. E. Morris 12-12-1877 (12-13-1877) [Ce]
Sterry, Tuck? to Amer E. Leigh 12-29-1880 (12-30-1880) [Ce]
Sterry?, William to Lucy H. Teasley 11-18-1871 (11-19-1871) [Ce]

Stewart, Arthur to Emma Binkley 6-23-1880   [Ce]
Stewart, Booker to Harriet Sheeran 12-28-1876 B [Ce]
Stewart, Charles to Margaret Baxter 1-24-1874 (3-8-1874) B [Ce]
Stewart, D. C. to Sarah W. Russell 12-18-1876 (12-24-1876) [Ce]
Stewart, Elijah A. to Martha E. Morgan 11-13-1866   [Ce]
Stewart, J. T. to M. J. Eatherly 10-13-1877 (10-14-1877) [Ce]
Stewart, J. W. to Margret Stewart 9-28-1869 (10-30-1869) [Ce]
Stewart, J.J. to Sarah P. Parry 11-16-1859 (11-17-1859) [Ce]
Stewart, Thos. J. to Mary T. A. Carter 10-20-1868 (10-22-1868)   [Ce]
Stewart, W. J. to Mary J. Edwards 12-28-1859   [Ce]
Stewart, W. M. to E. Majors 2-2-1866   [Ce]
Stovall, George M. to Tennessee Nicks 1-7-1869   [Ce]
Stringfellow, R. J. to E. A. Curfman 1-25-1862   [Ce]
Stringfellow, R. J. to Margret L. Stringfellow 10-24-1869   [Ce]
Stuart, A. W. to Ophelia McLaughlin 5-24-1879 (5-27-1879) [Ce]
Stuart, Charles M. to Emaline A. Symes 10-15-1859 (10-16-1859)   [Ce]
Stuart, J. R. to Mary J. Stewart 10-2-1871 (10-4-1871) [Ce]
Sullivean, J. F. to Mollie A. Griffin 10-10-1879   [Ce]
Sutton, John J. to Margret A. Crab 12-24-1870 (12-25-1870) [Ce]
Swan, R. M. to Mattie Stuart 2-19-1868 (2-20-1868) [Ce]
Swift, W. A. to Mary A. Jennett 10-12-1859 (10-13-1859) [Ce]
Swiney?, John to Gennie Hannah 9-21-1877 (9-22-1877) B [Ce]
Tally, D. B. S. to Nancy E. Stovall 12-3-1859   [Ce]
Taylor, Edward to Mary C. Cullum 12-15-1860 (12-16-1860) [Ce]
Taylor, Edwin to M. J. Deuling? 3-19-1877 (3-21-1877) [Ce]
Taylor, Elijah to Martha Andrews 2-13-1880 (2-15-1880) [Ce]
Taylor, Henry to Ema A. Andrews 6-29-1874 (7-1-1874) [Ce]
Teasley, Alexander to Elizabeth Harper 4-11-1868 (4-12-1868) [Ce]
Teasley, Benjamin to Sallie A. Teasley 1-30-1871 (2-2-1871) B [Ce]
Teasley, Charles to Alice Hooper 6-19-1880 (6-20-1880) B [Ce]
Teasley, Charter to Harriet Williams 1-27-1873 (1-30-1873) B [Ce]
Teasley, G. W. to Rebecca Jane Harris 9-18-1878 (9-19-1878) [Ce]
Teasley, J. E. to Mary Ann Sofrina Allbritten 12-12-1878   [Ce]
Teasley, John H. to Amelia A. Harris 9-30-1872 (10-3-1872) [Ce]
Teasley, L. F. to M. A. Wall 12-4-1866 (12-6-1866 [Ce]
Teasley, Lewis to Jennie Walton 6-9-1879 (6-13-1879) B [Ce]
Teasley, Mark to Levina Bell 4-3-1872 B [Ce]
Teasley, T. S. to M. T. Frey 10-15-1873 (10-16-1873) [Ce]
Teasley, Wm. E. to Nancy Hudgens 12-11-1869 (12-13-1869) [Ce]
Teasly, John M. to Tennessee Harper 12-6-1870 (12-7-1870) [Ce]
Teasly, W. to Rosetta Williams 2-8-1868 (2-22-1868) B [Ce]
Teline, O. L. to Huldy H. Dill 12-22-1868 (12-24-1868) [Ce]
Thomas, M. to Sarah E. Lowe 1-30-1866   [Ce]
Thompson, Allen T. to Alice M. Neal 2-13-1872 (2-15-1872) [Ce]
Thompson, E. E. to H. Simpson 1-12-1859 (1-13-1859) [Ce]
Thompson, J. B. to Rebecca B. Fulghum 5-11-1865 (5-18-1865) [Ce]
Thompson, Josephus to Cata Anderson 7-2-1873 (7-10-1873) B [Ce]
Thompson, Robert to Clarasy Hain? 1-28-1869 (1-29-1869) B [Ce]
Thompson, Samuel to Matilda Butler 10-20-1870 B [Ce]
Thompson, W. N. to Caroline R. Dunn 9-18-1872   [Ce]
Thompson, Wm. to Anner Easley 3-1-1877 B [Ce]
Thompson, Wm. W. to Susan A. Neal 12-6-1866   [Ce]
Thomson, P. C. to Emiline Lovell 10-15-1864   [Ce]
Thomson, S. W. to Emaline Hogue 8-23-1864   [Ce]

Tomlin, H. to Elizabeth Harrington 6-30-1877 (6-31?-1877) [Ce]
Travis, Andrew to Martha Wyatt 9-13-1873 (9-17-1873) [Ce]
True, J. W. to Sally Ann Jent 5-15-1862   [Ce]
Trulove, T. M. to N. E. McCorrall 7-25-1865 (7-26-1865) [Ce]
Turner, B. W. to Bettie Bell 12-3-1875   [Ce]
Turner, Charley M. to Allice Smith 3-8-1871   [Ce]
Turner, Daniel W. to Martha F. Erls 12-22-1870   [Ce]
Turner, Rufus to Harriett A. Riggan 1-5-1870 (1-6-1870) [Ce]
Turner, Thos. A. to Mary E. Pardue 11-22-1870 (11-23-1870) [Ce]
Turntine, W. M. to Mary J. Binkley 12-7-1865   [Ce]
Twiner, M. G. to M. E. Frazier 10-27-1880 (10-28-1880) [Ce]
Tyson, John to Sarah Elizabeth Guptono 4-22-1879 (4-23-1879)   [Ce]
Ussery, Colman to Amanda Gorden 3-19-1873 B [Ce]
Ussery, Jarmin to Mary Hannah 12-23-1874 B [Ce]
Ussery, William to Nancy Dozier 5-23-1864   [Ce]
Van Vaulkinburgh, Isaac to Mary Perkins 9-1-1873   [Ce]
Vanhook, J. D. to Mary L. Fox 1-26-1861 (1-27-1861) [Ce]
Vanhook, J. D. to Sarah Wilson 8-3-1857   [Ce]
Varden, Elisha to Nancy E. Crawford 1-21-1869 (2-4-1869) [Ce]
Vaughan, J. P. to Sarah V. Malory 6-15-1861 (6-18-1861) [Ce]
Vaughn, Johnson to Eliza Berry 1-7-1859 (1-11-1859) [Ce]
Ventress, A. J. to U.? Harrington 3-10-1859 (3-30-1859) [Ce]
Ventress, Thos. R. to Nancy J. Council 8-13-1864   [Ce]
Vick, J. P. to Delilah Ryman 12-30-1879   [Ce]
Vick, Wm. R. to Alice E. N. Hunt 1-23-1879   [Ce]
Viverett, J. M. to Sallie D. Lowe 2-20-1879   [Ce]
Walker, A. M. to S. A. Binkley 10-26-1859   [Ce]
Walker, Adam to Ann Mariah Williams 12-30-1873 B [Ce]
Walker, Alert to Melissa Hunt 4-13-1878 (4-14-1878) B [Ce]
Walker, Carril to Dethed Edwards 1-5-1866 B [Ce]
Walker, Ed to Mary Hampton 3-2-1879 B [Ce]
Walker, Ed to Mary Hampton 3-2-1879 B [Ce]
Walker, Hardridge to Martha K. Williams 1-18-1860 (1-19-1860)   [Ce]
Walker, Henry to Fillis Ann Watson 2-2-1878 (2-3-1878) B [Ce]
Walker, J. D. to Martha Weakley 2-5-1881 (2-13-1881) [Ce]
Walker, J. T. to Martha Woodall 4-11-1878 (4-14-1878) [Ce]
Walker, James R. to A. E. Lanier 4-23-1873   [Ce]
Walker, James W. to Susan Walker 9-9-1868   [Ce]
Walker, John to Eliza Bell 8-24-1866 (9-1-1866) B [Ce]
Walker, John to Jane S. Neal 11-25-1865 B [Ce]
Walker, John T. to George Ann Burford 1-18-1877 (1-21-1877)   [Ce]
Walker, Joshua to Jenney Willi9ams 5-18-1874 B [Ce]
Walker, Leander to George A. S. Edwards 6-4-1868   [Ce]
Walker, M. C. to Amy Council 2-22-1871 B [Ce]
Walker, M. V. B. to F. Murphy 2-10-1858   [Ce]
Walker, Scott to Hannah Wall 7-27-1872 (7-27-1872) B [Ce]
Walker, T. E. to Nancy Teasley 1-3-1876   [Ce]
Walker, Thomas to Celary George Ann Edwards 12-29-1878   [Ce]
Walker, Thomas to Delvira George Ann Harris (no dates)   [Ce]
Walker, W. C. to Lucy Lenox 2-7-1880 (2-8-1880) B [Ce]
Walker, W. H. to Mary W. Maxey 12-4-1879   [Ce]
Walker, W. M. to Francis Mitchel 12-20-1878 (12-24-1878) [Ce]
Walker, William to R. J. Gray 11-25-1858 (12-1-1858) [Ce]
Walker, Z. T. to Susan A. Wilson 4-21-1875 (4-22-1875) [Ce]

Walkins, William to Margret Watson 3-25-1869 B [Ce]
Walkup, James to Billie F. Pegram 12-3-1860 (12-20-1860) [Ce]
Wall, David A. to Elmina Sanders 1-13-1874   [Ce]
Wall, G. W. to P. T. Teasley 3-29-1876 (3-30-1876) [Ce]
Wall, J. H. to H. R. Shearon 2-8-1881 (2-9-1881) [Ce]
Wall, James D. to Mary E. Walker 12-18-1877   [Ce]
Wall, Solomon to Emma Speight 8-18-1877 B [Ce]
Wall, Wm. H. to M. A. H. Maxey 1-6-1876   [Ce]
Waller, B. W. to Mamie Williams 2-3-1872 (2-7-1872) [Ce]
Walls, J. T. to Emily Justice 2-28-1878   [Ce]
Walton, Robert to Lucretia Bobo 1-13-1866 (1-20-1866) B [Ce]
Warner, W. W. to E. R. Ferrell 10-4-1858   [Ce]
Washington, George to Mary Drake? 2-18-1881 (2-19-1881) B [Ce]
Washington, Saml. to Martha Washington 12-16-1869 (12-26-1869) B [Ce]
Washington, Samuel to Sefrona Robertson 10-13-1877 B [Ce]
Washington, Thomas to Virginia Patterson 6-13-1876 B [Ce]
Waters?, Wm. to Nancy Coan? 11-29-1879 (11-30-1879) [Ce]
Watkins, A. C. to Louisanna Lovell 12-27-1859 (1-1-1860) [Ce]
Watkins, David to Susan Farlen 10-30-1875 (10-21?-1876?) B [Ce]
Watkins, S. J. to Julia Stump? 10-17-1866   [Ce]
Watkins, Samuel D. to Christianna Stump 2-27-1873 (3-2-1873) [Ce]
Watson, Clarence to L. Hooper 10-13-1867 (10-20-1867) B [Ce]
Watson, Jordan to Julia Watson 12-24-1866 (12-27-1866) B [Ce]
Watson, Lee to Martha J. Shafara? 12-2-1880 [Ce]
Watson, Richard to Harriet Mallory 2-28-1873 (3-1-1873) B [Ce]
Watts, J.F. to Mary Stack 3-20-1876 (3-29-1876) [Ce]
Watts, R. J. to Fredonia Miles 11-12-1879 (11-6?-1879) [Ce]
Weakley, Benjamin L. to Lousianna T. Chambliss 10-14-1875   [Ce]
Weakley, Clay to Fannie Lankford 6-22-1881 (6-23-1881) B [Ce]
Weakley, Robert to Ann Davis 12-14-1867 (12-17-1867) [Ce]
Weakley, Wm. D. to Nancy J. Teasley 1-12-1859 (1-13-1859) [Ce]
Weakly, G. W. to Alis Balthrop 1-6-1868   [Ce]
Webb, M. W. to Mary Miles 9-4-1876   [Ce]
Wells, George to Mary Mallery 9-12-1866 (9-20-1866) B [Ce]
Wheeler, Ed A. to M. M. Stack 5-28-1858 (6-4-1858) [Ce]
White, Isaac to L. Carter 8-2-1865 B [Ce]
White, R. H. to R. S. Basford 12-18-1875 (12-26-1875) [Ce]
White, Robert to Emily Lee 8-14-1873 B [Ce]
White, Spencer to Edy Cooper 1-2-1872 (1-4-1872) B [Ce]
Whitehead, Jacob to Elizabeth Pennington 1-24-1870 (1-30-1870) [Ce]
Whitworth, W. to Mary T. Nicholson 8-7-1880 (8-15-1880) [Ce]
Whitworth, Wm. H. to Martha J. Jackson 6-21-1866 (6-25-1866) [Ce]
Wilkins, C. A. to P.? C. Hunt 12-2-1867 (12-11?-1867) [Ce]
Williams, Aaron to Celia Felts 7-4-1866 B [Ce]
Williams, Alford to Parile Thompson 5-1-1875 B [Ce]
Williams, Benj. to Geraline Hunter 12-28-1867 (7-11-1868) B [Ce]
Williams, C. F. to Harriet York 10-28-1874   [Ce]
Williams, F. W. to M. J. Harding 7-8-1865   [Ce]
Williams, G. W. to Martha C. Watt 11-20-1878 (no return) [Ce]
Williams, George to Mary Boyd 9-14-1872 (9-25-1872) B [Ce]
Williams, Henry to Mary J. Batson 1-25-1871 B [Ce]
Williams, Henry T. to Jennie A. Rosson 4-29-1870   [Ce]
Williams, J. B. to Mary R. Henderson 10-18-1880 (10-21-1880) [Ce]
Williams, J. R. to Esther Ann R. Jackson 10-5-1872 (10-6-1872) [Ce]

Williams, J. W. to Martha Hooper 6-13-1874 (6-14-1874) [Ce]
Williams, James to Virginia Denney 3-24-1869 (3-25-1869) [Ce]
Williams, Mark to Hennie Washington 8-23-1879 B [Ce]
Williams, Moses to Amy Teasley 1-21-1873 B [Ce]
Williams, Moses to Marina Balthrop 12-29-1877 (12-30-1877) B [Ce]
Williams, P. C. to D. A. Edwards 1-16-1860 [Ce]
Williams, Perry to Shosie Shearon 5-?-1880 B [Ce]
Williams, Peter to Sallie Hunter 4-17-1876 (4-20-1876) B [Ce]
Williams, R. W. to Mary Robertson 10-6-1869 [Ce]
Williams, R. W. to R. Coleman 7-6-1858 [Ce]
Williams, Richard to Rebecca Colnon 11-28-1865 [Ce]
Williams, Thos. J. to Harriet Harris 4-5-1869 [Ce]
Williams, W. A. to M. C. Dismukes 1-14-1865 [Ce]
Williams, Wm. to Lou Everett 1-2-1874 B [Ce]
Williams, __. to Rebecca P. Lovell 10-27-1859 [Ce]
Willis, Wilson to Susan T. Willis 10-24-1870 (10-25-1870) [Ce]
Wilson, Amos R. to Marana V. Jones 9-24-1866 (9-27-1866) [Ce]
Wilson, Coral? to Sopia White 3-3-1880 (3-4-1880) B [Ce]
Wilson, Green T. to Emma Bradley 8-16-1879 [Ce]
Wilson, Isaac to Mary N. Sanders 12-23-1869 [Ce]
Wilson, J. J. to Loucretia Rudelph 1-6-1874 (1-8-1874) [Ce]
Wilson, J. W. to Almedia Teasley 3-2-1872 (3-3-1872) [Ce]
Wilson, J.M. to Emily Edwards 3-19-1881 (3-20-1881) B [Ce]
Wilson, James T. to Virginia T. Gossett 11-11-1868 (11-13-1868) [Ce]
Wilson, Lewis H. to Sarah Ford 6-22-1867 (6-28-1867) [Ce]
Wilson, Peter to Caroline Vanhook 10-6-1866 B [Ce]
Wilson, Peter to Ellen McGowen 8-1-1879 B [Ce]
Wilson, Robt. to Jane Birthright 10-31-1877 (11-2-1877) B [Ce]
Winters, J. W. to M. E. Bradley 12-23-1871 (12-24-1871) [Ce]
Winters, M. W. to Elizabeth J. Cochran 2-26-1877 (3-1-1877) [Ce]
Woodall, Wilie to Mary Felts 7-17-1872 (7-18-1872) [Ce]
Woodmoore, Samel to Lou Jackson 7-26-1875 (7-27-1874?) B [Ce]
Woodmore?, Jerre to Clen? Huddleston 2-7-1880 (3-28-1880) B [Ce]
Woods, Z. A. to Edima? Williams 11-6-1880 (11-7-1880) B [Ce]
Woodson, Elijah to Caroline Farmer 4-16-1869 (4-17-1869) B [Ce]
Woodson, J. T. to Nancy J. McDaniel 6-26-1875 [Ce]
Woodson, Maro to Ida Jenkins 1-26-1881 (1-27-1881) [Ce]
Woodson, T. A. to Mary? E. Hooper 12-29-1870 (1-3-1871) [Ce]
Woodward, Ephraim to Sarah Newsom 1-2-1874 (1-3-1874) B [Ce]
Woodward, G. P. to S. E. Smith 6-8-1861 (6-9-1861) [Ce]
Woodward, Leonard to Eliza Brown 12-26-1867 (1-19-1868) B [Ce]
Woodward, Thomas to Amanda Ussery 9-18-1876 (9-26-1876) B [Ce]
Work, William L. to Susan A. Davis 10-25-1873 (10-26-1873) [Ce]
Worthey, Green to E. J. Griggsby 3-4-1863 [Ce]
Worthy, Green to E. J. Grigsby 3-4-1863 [Ce]
Wren, E. T. to L. A. Woodall 12-21-1858 (12-23-1858) [Ce]
Wright, B. F. to Eliza Basford 1-17-1861 [Ce]
Wright, Joseph M. to Arlie Bennett 1-6-1875 [Ce]
Wyatt, M. S. to Bettie Tomlin 5-5-1874 [Ce]
Wyndham, G. G. to Nancy F. Ussery 12-19-1866 [Ce]
Yates, Joseph to Priscilla Greer 1-16-1875 (1-21-1875) [Ce]
Yates, William to Mary Greer 2-6-1862 [Ce]
York, J. C. to Rosanna Sherron 11-23-1872 (11-24-1872) [Ce]
Young, B. F. to Martha A. Carney 9-30-1864 [Ce]

Young, James to Susan Edwards? 3-15-1865   [Ce]
Young, James to Susan T. Newman 2-17-1865   [Ce]
_____, Ellis to Mamma Jones 1-2-1867 (1-13-1867) B [Ce]

Abanathey, Frances E. to C. A. Oakley 1-16-1875 (1-18-1875)
Abanathy, Elizabeth to Jerry Maxwell 7-30-1867 (8-1-1867)
Abanathy, Mary L. to Thos. J. Carney 8-12-1871
Adams, G. A. to E. E. Evans 10-2-1879
Adcock, E. to W. L. Bright 7-8-1865 (7-16-1865)
Adcock, Julia to John Knight 1-29-1877
Adkins, H. A. to G. S. Pickering 1-31-1858
Adkins, H. A. to G. S. Pickering no date (with May 1858)
Adkins, Mary M. to Samuel Clifton 5-10-1856
Akin, Sarah Ann Jane to Robert Murphey 5-27-1871 (5-29-1871)
Allbritten, Mary Ann Sofrina to J. E. Teasley 12-12-1878
Allen, Sallie S. to D. W. Stack 12-23-1879
Allen, Susanah to James R. Hamilton 10-1-1874
Allen, Thursey R. to C. J. Perdue 10-28-1873 (10-30-1873)
Allen?, Mattie to John A. King 12-24-1870 (12-25-1870)
Allers, Sarah A. to G. R. Fox? 10-11-1876 (10-12-1876)
Alley, E. A. to R. Moore 8-25-1859
Alley, Emily to John A. Edgin 9-?-1858 (9-29-1858)
Alley, Marth J. to Benja. J. Stack 4-11-1857
Alley, Martha A. to Charles E. Anderson 9-16-1874 (9-20-1874)
Alley, Nora P. to Wm. H. Hooper 12-13-1873 (12-14-1873)
Alley, S. A. to W. J. Gray 2-3-1858 (2-4-1858)
Anderson, Bettie to S. Daniel 6-30-1877 (7-1-1877) B
Anderson, Cata to Josephus Thompson 7-2-1873 (7-10-1873) B
Anderson, Laura to William Bratton 12-10-1863
Anderson, Luvina to William Knight 3-25-1874 (3-27-1874) B
Anderson, Margaret to John Harris 7-19-1871 (7-22-1871)
Anderson, Mary J. to Clay Roberts 8-12-1875
Anderson, Mollie to James Perry 4-1-1880
Anderson, Pauline to Len Robertson 9-18-1880 B
Anderson, Sarah to James L. Samples 9-26-1868 (10-1-1868)
Andrews, Ema A. to Henry Taylor 6-29-1874 (7-1-1874)
Andrews, Martha to Elijah Taylor 2-13-1880 (2-15-1880)
Andrews, Mary A. to William Creech 3-21-1861
Andrews, Mary E. to G. W. Balum 2-20-1879 (2-23-1879) B
Arington, Catharine to James M. Binkley 6-29-1864
Atkison, Mary to Wm. H. H. Forrest 1-8-1876 B
Bagwell, Emma M. to John H. W. Greer 1-25-1875 (1-26-1875)
Bailey, Emily to J. H. Perry 12-29-1857 (12-30-1857)
Baker, Mary to W. T. McDaniel 6-30-1879 (7-1-1879)
Ballard, Maggie to William Page 1-21-1880 (1-22-1880)
Balthrop, Alis to G. W. Weakly 1-6-1868
Balthrop, Augusta H. to Edward Hewitt 10-19-1874 (10-20-1874)
Balthrop, M. A. to John O. Hunter 8-7-1858 (8-10-1858)
Balthrop, Marina to Moses Williams 12-29-1877 (12-30-1877) B
Bames, H. to D. S. Collins 1-7-1857 (1-8-1857)
Barclift, Ellic to John Pegram 5-31-1870 (6-19-1870) B
Barclift, M. E. to Sam F. Glass 5-30-1860
Barnes, Catie to Charlie T. Biggs 4-28-1879
Barnes, S. D. A. to W. H. Knight 9-25-1880 (9-26-1880)
Barton, Mary to Jobe Collins 1-14-1874 (1-16-1874) B
Barton, Mary to Hardy Grant 4-6-1872 B
Barton, Permeld to Taylor Elliott 12-25-1872 (12-26-1872) B

Barton, Tennessee to Wm. B. Cross 8-14-1856
Basford, Eliza to B. F. Wright 1-17-1861
Basford, Martha to George Major 12-18-1869 (12-23-1869)
Basford, R. S. to R. H. White 12-18-1875 (12-26-1875)
Batsen, Narcissa to Jno. A. Edgin 6-6-1877 (6-8-1877)
Batson, Emaline to Ruffin Nicholson 3-2-1872 (3-7-1872) B
Batson, Mary J. to Henry Williams 1-25-1871 B
Batson, Mollie to charley Council 2-8-1881 B
Bawsel, H. A. to B. J. Edwards 3-3-1873 (3-4-1873)
Baxter, Margaret to Charles Stewart 1-24-1874 (3-8-1874) B
Beach, Victoria A. to William J. Gunter 12-18-1879
Bearden, Eliz. to John B. Cain 9-29-1858
Bearden, Nancy to B. H. Frazier 1-12-1858 (1-14-1858)
Beck, Tennessee to Charles Ferebee 12-18-1871 (12-23-1871) B
Beggar, Mahala to Drue Hunter 7-13-1881 B
Bell, Annie to J. W. Carney 3-2-1881
Bell, Bettie to B. W. Turner 12-3-1875
Bell, C. O. to R. E. Douglas 9-27-1860 (9-28-1860)
Bell, Chaerty? to Alexr. Hale 9-3-1866 (9-6-1866) B
Bell, Eliza to John Walker 8-24-1866 (9-1-1866) B
Bell, Levina to Mark Teasley 4-3-1872 B
Bell, Lilly to George Adkisson 12-24-1878 B
Bell, Martha to Aleck Clark 10-13-1870 B
Bell, Martha to Rubin Sayer 3-2-1878 (3-3-1878) B
Bell, Patsey to Ruben Sayers 11-24-1877 B
Bell, R. C. to Sam Y. Brown 3-2-1859 (3-3-1859)
Bell, Sarah E. to William Gupton 10-14-1873 (10-13?-1873)
Benefield, Phereby to Samuel Sells 3-26-1867 (3-28-1867)
Bennett, Arlie to Joseph M. Wright 1-6-1875
Bennett, Mary to Montgomery Binkley 1-23-1858 (1-24-1858)
Bennett, Mary T. to O. H. Dickerson 12-2-1858 (12-5-1858)
Bennett, Susanah E. to Thos. S. Henn? 12-22-1857
Bennett, Tabitha to Leonard Binkley 8-16-1862
Bennett, Tennessee to Richard Reding 3-13-1867 (3-19-1867)
Benningfield, Nancy to Peter Andrews 4-19-1875
Benton, Eliza J. to A. J. Rinehart 9-19-1876 (9-21-1876)
Berry, Eliza to Johnson Vaughn 1-7-1859 (1-11-1859)
Berry, Mary N. to Joel F. Mays 12-7-1857 (12-10-1857)
Berthrite, Pat to Lorenzo Lewis 4-24-1880 (4-25-1880) B
Betis, Sarah to John Obearr 3-17-1864
Bidwell, Sarah J. to John Foster 9-28-1867 (10-12-1867) B
Bigger, Mary J. to John R. Pace 1-16-1867 (1-17-1867)
Biggs, Caroline to Phillip Brooks 3-21-1874 (3-22-1874)
Biggs, Elizabeth to Allen Cagle 1-13-1869
Biggs, Julia A. to J. L. Simpkins 2-4-1874 (2-6-1874)
Biggs, Mary to Jasper Marewell 12-24-1867 (12-25-1867)
Biggs, Sarah A. to J. S. Demumbra 8-7-1874 (8-8-1874)
Binkley, A. to R. Lee 12-23-1856 (12-25-1856)
Binkley, Angeline to Joshua W. Morris 12-27-1876 (12-28-1876)
Binkley, Dibra to J. H. Head 11-4-1867 (11-7-1867)
Binkley, Emma to Jeff Anglin 5-25-1881 B
Binkley, Emma to Arthur Stewart 6-23-1880
Binkley, Frances to Stephen Mayo 10-17-1877
Binkley, George A. to J. M. Babb 8-17-1874 (8-19-1874)

Binkley, H. J. to D. J. Fetts 1-4-1858
Binkley, Harriet to J. C. B. Rose 5-26-1866 (5-31-1866)
Binkley, Harriet D. to John Boyd 10-19-1867
Binkley, Julia A. to B. J. Barnes 11-18-1858
Binkley, Katharine to John R. Binkley 12-10-1857
Binkley, L. A. to W. A. Edgin 1-18-1865
Binkley, Lavina to William M. Carney 2-6-1867 (2-7-1867)
Binkley, Lou to J. A. Felts 6-14-1879
Binkley, Lucind to George Binkley 8-18-1871   B
Binkley, Lucy A. to F. G. Boyt 2-13-1861
Binkley, M. A. E. to W. T. Sanders 9-11-1864
Binkley, Martha to Monroe Binkley 8-2-1866
Binkley, Martha to J. W. Demumbra 6-16-1876 (6-18-1876)
Binkley, Mary to Thos. F. Bell 11-5-1863
Binkley, Mary to Wm. P. Cagle 2-3-1876
Binkley, Mary to Thomas J. Farmer 10-20-1871 (10-22-1871)
Binkley, Mary to Wm. Rudeker 10-9-1857
Binkley, Mary J. to W. M. Turntine 12-7-1865
Binkley, Nancy A. to Thomas McCommack 7-19-1859 (7-21-1859)
Binkley, Nancy Ann to H. L. Morris 10-2-1869 (10-3-1869)
Binkley, Parlee to Felix G. Boyte 3-9-1868 (6-14-1868)
Binkley, S. A. to A. M. Walker 10-26-1859
Binkley, Sarah to W. H. Powell 9-18-1872 (9-19-1872)
Binkley, Susan to Thos. A. Newlen 7-15-1864
Binkley, T. M. to B. H. Nabors 8-17-1861
Birthright, Jane to Robt. Wilson 10-31-1877 (11-2-1877) B
Birthright, Martha to William Boyd 12-19-1877 (12-27-1877)
Blain, Sarah to F. M. Copley 3-7-1860 (5-16-1860)
Blane, Nancy to John Guthrie 1-16-1867 (1-17-1867)
Blankenship, Martha J. to N. L. Greene 10-19-1874
Bledsoe, Susa to Silas Greer 10-8-1866 (11-6-1866)
Bobbett, Virginia to Stephen Bobbett 12-6-1859
Bobbitt, Eller D. to Joseph Hand 2-27-1878
Bobbitt, Nancy M. to W. W. Smith 12-30-1871 (1-4-1872)
Bobbitt, Q. R. to J. H. Outlaw? 5-8-880 (5-9-1880)
Bobo, Lucretia to Robert Walton 1-13-1866 (1-20-1866) B
Bone, Mary A. to C. W. Anderson 3-7-1861
Bonnett, Lu to Frank A. Anderson 8-22-1871
Boyd, E. C. to C. C. Darrow 12-24-1877
Boyd, Ellen to Bynam G. Neighbors 10-14-1871 (10-15-1871)
Boyd, M. E. to E. A. Noe 12-17-1877 (12-18-1877)
Boyd, M. M. to H. G. Nicholson 2-3-1877 (2-5-1877)
Boyd, Mary to R. W. Demumbra 6-24-1871
Boyd, Mary to George Williams 9-14-1872 (9-25-1872) B
Boyd, Mary Isabelle to A. F. Binkley 12-20-1873 (12-26-1873)
Boyd, Nelia to Wm. T. Bright 10-21-1869 (10-22-1869)
Boyd, Susan F. to James I. Simpkins 9-25-1875 (9-26-1875)
Boyde, Hulda to James R. W. Cochran 4-9-1881 (4-17-1881)
Boyle, Sarah J. to E. W. Smith 12-29-1880 (12-30-1880)
Boyt, Elizabeth to Robt. Parthene 10-27-1869 (10-28-1869)
Boyte, Cornelia to Jos. E. Sanders 2-26-1881 (2-27-1881)
Boyte, Martha J. to William B. Martin 4-13-1878 (no return)
Boyte, Parelee to W. C. Samples 8-28-1874
Bracy, Mary to Isaac W. Alley 12-25-1857

Bradford, Mary E. to W. C. Lovell 7-6-1868
Bradford, Tennessee to John Jordan 10-9-1873 B
Bradley, Emma to Green T. Wilson 8-16-1879
Bradley, Lieu to Richard Hyde 11-18-1879 (11-19-1879) B
Bradley, M. E. to J. W. Winters 12-23-1871 (12-24-1871)
Bradley, Virginia C. to W. S. Lockert 2-14-1878
Bratton, Lorey to William Lyles 8-2-1878 (8-4-1878)
Bright, Ann M. to Thos. L. Gray 11-30-1857 (12-9-1857)
Bright, Mary Ella to Thomopson Biggar 1-6-1879 (1-8-1879)
Brinkley, A. to W. T. Miller 1-2-1858 (1-3-1858)
Brinkley, Catharine to John B. Demumbra 3-17-1860 (3-18-1860)
Brinkley, D. M. to Jno. L. W. Power 1-6-1881
Brinkley, Georgia to William A. Eatherly 1-15-1874
Brinkley, H. J. to David J. Fetts 1-4-1858
Brinkley, Josephine E. to Robert W. Hooper 5-31-1869 (6-1-1869)
Brinkley, M. to Henry J. Carney 12-29-1857
Brinkley, M. A. to W. F. Follis 3-7-1861
Brinkley, Sarah C. to James N. Osburn 4-5-1859 (4-4?-1859)
Brinkley, Susan J. to James S. Hollis 2-27-1861 (2-28-1861)
Brown, Adar R. to John A. Mays 9-24-1872
Brown, Almier to W. L. Lovell 7-20-1881
Brown, Cherry to George Harris 12-18-1874 B
Brown, E. H. to W. C. Neal 1-4-1879 (1-5-1879)
Brown, Eliza to Leonard Woodward 12-26-1867 (1-19-1868) B
Brown, Maggie to Burrell Jackson 3-5-1877 (3-7-1877)
Brown, Mary J. to L. W. jr. Lovell 2-28-1877
Brown, Mary Jane to Bursell Edwards 7-17-1868 (7-18-1868
Brown, R. C. to J. M. Martin 3-2-1867
Brown, Rebecca to S. H. Cearley 4-24-1869 (4-29-1869)
Brown, Sarah S. to J. H. Carney 12-31-1872 (1-1-1873)
Brunrack?, M. A. to W. W. Morris 2-18-1879 (2-23-1879)
Bryant, Nancy C. to Wm. S. Burgess 6-5-1869 (6-6-1869)
Buckley, Anna J. to J. H. Felts 3-21-1878 (3-24-1878)
Buckley, Eliza to W. A. Gallaher 10-9-1875 (10-10-1875)
Buckley, Louisa to Wilson Boyd 1-14-1878
Buckley, Virginia L. to L. H. Hicks 10-21-1872 (10-23-1872)
Bundy?, Malvina to G. J. Carney 1-21-1877
Burford, George Ann to John T. Walker 1-18-1877 (1-21-1877)
Burkley, Mary E. to Franklin Ford 12-24-1877 (12-25-1877)
Burrow, Susan to James Elrod 7-27-1865 B
Burton, Roena to Robert Collins 8-13-1879 (8-14-1879) B
Bush, Lucinda to Moses McCree 3-18-1869 B
Butler, Delila to Jerry Hale 1-11-1867 (1-13-1867) B
Butler, Matilda to Samuel Thompson 10-20-1870 B
Butts, Mary E. to J. H. Mays? 11-8-1876 (11-23-1876)
Cagle, Elisa A. to J. W. Demumbra 1-7-1873 (1-9-1873)
Cagle, Mandelia to James S. Binkley 12-14-1872 (12-19-1872)
Cagle, Marina to Robert Crantz 1-25-1866
Cagle, Rosetta to J. T. Barnes 5-25-1876
Cagle, Susan C. to William Goodwin 4-14-1857 (4-16-1857)
Cain, Eliz. to M. Nicholson 12-27-1856
Cain, Julia M. to John Perdue 10-21-1858
Caral, Ruth to Wm. J. Ham 12-4-1869 (12-5-1869)
Carney, Ellata to Geo. F. Murff 5-14-1878 (5-16-1878)

4

Carney, Maggie J. to Maxo? Felts 11-25-1878 (11-26-1878)
Carney, Martha A. to B. F. Young 9-30-1864
Carney, Mary to Laban Abanathy 2-27-1865
Carney, Mollie J. to Arther A. Sloan 12-21-1880 (12-22-1880)
Carney, Nancy J. to Geo. W. Boyd 6-28-1876 (6-29-1876)
Carney, S. P. to John J. Mays 6-21-1862
Carney, Tabitha to Lenard Binkley 12-16-1858
Carney, Unis C. to John F. Friendsley 2-3-1873 (2-7-1873)
Carneye, Alise to Geo. W. Chadion 6-13-1878
Carpenter, Lutitia T. to J. D. Darrow 10-14-1874
Carson, Alice C. to W. T. Perry 4-12-1866
Carter, L. to Isaac White 8-2-1865 B
Carter, M. P. to J. P. Bell 9-26-1879
Carter, Mary T. A. to Thos. J. Stewart 10-20-1868 (10-22-1868)
Carter, Thena to Sill Pegram 4-3-1872 (4-7-1872) B
Casey, Elvira to G. W. Harris 10-4-1860 (12-10-1860)
Casey, Malinda to Hiram D. Fitts 5-27-1857
Casey, Narcissy to Levi Simmons 12-29-1857
Casey, Susan F. to William Hooper 10-23-1861
Cate?, Sarah J. to A. Stalcup 12-30-1867
Cato?, Amanda to Wesley Edwards 12-25-1871 B
Ceerby, Mary to Wm. E. Kenney 9-12-1873
Chadowin, Ann to William Littrell 7-14-1879 (7-17-1879)
Chambliss, E. A. to G. W. Johnson 10-22-1879 (10-23-1879)
Chambliss, Emily T. to Joshua B. Major 10-14-1868 (10-15-1868)
Chambliss, Julia to Edward Ramer 12-2-1880
Chambliss, Lousianna T. to Benjamin L. Weakley 10-14-1875
Chambliss, M. A. to Geo. Knight 11-14-1860 (11-16-1860)
Chambliss, Perlina F. to Rufus M. Felts 3-31-1869 (4-1-1869)
Chambliss, R. B. to N. T. Nicholson 9-26-1876 (9-27-1876)
Chambliss, Sarah to Robert Barton 1-27-1873 (1-30-1873) B
Charlton, Emer to Henry Holt 7-6-1878 (7-8-1878) B
Charlton, Molly A. to Joseph F. Mays 1-19-1877 (1-23-1877)
Chase, Adaline to Carroll Hamilton 9-22-1877 B
Chase, Mariah to Aron Brown 2-24-1881 (2-26-1881) B
Chase, Rutha to Charles Harris 12-5-1868 (12-13-1868) B
Cheatham, Eliza to Frank Lane 1-3-1868 B
Cheatham, Elizabeth to F. Cheatham 1-5-1868 B
Christy, Mallinda to H. J. Groves 10-14-1878 (10-20-1878)
Christy, Martha J. to Jas. W. Hampton 5-5-1879 (5-7-1879)
Clark, A. A. to H. C. Miles 6-28-1861 (6-20-1861)
Clark, Adaline F. to William P. Redd 2-13-1863
Clark, Josephine to Charles R. Shadowen 7-21-1879
Clark, Lilly to John Farmer 3-12-1881 (3-13-1881)
Clark, P. I. to C. H. Appleton 6-11-1860 (6-14-1860)
Clark, Polly to Berge Finley 4-19-1867 B
Clifton, Ann E. to John M. Nanney 1-3-1870 (1-9-1870)
Clifton, Mary to Lemuel Davis 1-5-1870 (1-6-1870)
Clinard, Delia to Joseph Chambliss 2-28-1878 (3-1-1878)
Clinard, Sarah to Wm. Scruggs 10-16-1876 (10-18-1876)
Coan?, Nancy to Wm. Waters? 11-29-1879 (11-30-1879)
Cochran, Elizabeth J. to M. W. Winters 2-26-1877 (3-1-1877)
Cochran, Mary L. to W. T. Farmer 8-7-1876 (8-17-1876)
Cole, Lucy to Robt. S. Garvits? 3-9-1881 (3-11-1881) B

Coleman, Loucinda to James Cain 1-12-1860
Coleman, Martha to Augustus Bearden 6-2-1858 (6-3-1858)
Coleman, Parthenia to Hiram L. Jones 12-27-1870 (12-29-1870)
Coleman, R. to R. W. Williams 7-6-1858
Collier, Caroline to Charles Collier 5-18-1872 (5-20-1872) B
Collins, Amanda to John C. Collins 3-20-1860 (3-21-1860)
Collins, Luan to Geo. A. Eleazor 8-24-1860 (8-26-1860)
Collins, Lucinda to Green M. Collins 3-28-1862
Colnon, Rebecca to Richard Williams 11-28-1865
Comperry, P. to John A. Pool 6-14-1859
Cooper, Edy to Spencer White 1-2-1872 (1-4-1872) B
Cooper, Julia to Phillip Adkisson 9-16-1867 (9-23-1867) B
Cooper, Pheby J. F. to G. A. Scott 1-20-1881
Cothen, Sarah J. to Isaac W. Read 11-12-1863 (11-18-1863)
Council, Amy to Willis Harris 11-28-1867 B
Council, Amy to M. C. Walker 2-22-1871 B
Council, Mary E. to E. T. Clifton 5-16-1859
Council, Nancy J. to Thos. R. Ventress 8-13-1864
Council, P. W. to C. W. Murphy 11-1-1869
Cox, Darcus to Alexander Hale 6-20-1868 B
Crab, Margret A. to John J. Sutton 12-24-1870 (12-25-1870)
Craighead, Racheal to Jessee Heyde 2-21-1877 (2-26-1877) B
Crawford, Nancy E. to Elisha Varden 1-21-1869 (2-4-1869)
Crider, Emily to Phillip H. Mitchel 2-1-1879 (2-5-1879)
Critts, Frances to George Lyttle 3-12-1868
Croach, Virginia T. to D. M. Jordan 12-26-1861
Crockett, Susan to H. Dozier 12-27-1876 B
Cross, Sarah J. to C. C. Pakins 4-17-1857 (4-21-1857)
Crouch, Ann to James N. Hooper 10-8-1872 (10-9-1872)
Crouch, L. M. to A. B. Lovell 7-22-1861 (7-25-1861)
Crouch, Nancy to William Brown 5-4-1871 (5-15-1871)
Crowder, Jane to George Johnson 12-16-1878 B
Crumpler, Bettie to A. P. Corlew 8-31-1881
Crumpler, Dora E. to M. J. Crumpler 3-17-1863
Crumpler, Martha to William Howell 7-28-1864
Cullum, Harriet to J. H. Lovell 1-23-1869 (1-27-1869)
Cullum, M. C. to J. O. Hooper 12-8-1865
Cullum, Martha to William Bristow 11-14-1859 (11-17-1859)
Cullum, Mary C. to Edward Taylor 12-15-1860 (12-16-1860)
Cullum, Nancy C. to David W. Nichols 6-4-1870 (6-5-1870)
Cullum, Tennie to W. C. Clark 7-2-1860
Curfman, E. A. to R. J. Stringfellow 1-25-1862
Curfman, E. E. (Mrs.) to F. P. Lovell 12-14-1871 (12-19-1871)
Curfman, M. E. to E. W. Pack 12-22-1875 (12-26-1875)
Curfner, L. L. to J. W. Buchanan 1-8-1881 (1-10-1881)
Curtis, Mandy to Jerry Hamlin 12-25-1878 (12-26-1878) B
Daily, E.J. to John D. Hill 8-3-1863
Darden, Harriet to Silas Dickerson 5-25-1867 (6-1-1867) B
Darrow, Martha to J. K. P. Mosier 8-10-1865
Darrow, Rosa E. to Wm. W. Harris 5-18-1874 (6-7-1874)
Davis, Ann to Robert Weakley 12-14-1867 (12-17-1867)
Davis, Martha E. to T. R. Friendsly 7-26-1876 (7-27-1876)
Davis, Mary D. to Alexander Galloway 12-25-1874
Davis, Susan A. to William L. Work 10-25-1873 (10-26-1873)

Deal, Mary to William T. Deal 1-16-1875
Demumbra, A. to Lewis Dickerson 5-15-1876
Demumbra, M. A. T. to S. T. Abanathy 7-14-1857
Demumbra, M. A. T. to S. Y. Abanathy 7-14-1857 (7-17-1857)
Demumbra, Martha to C. J. C. Shivers 5-27-1876 (5-28-1876)
Demumbra, Melinda to eorge Mayer 12-10-1857 (12-11-1857)
Demumbra, Milly to William Neighbors 6-8-1874
Demumbra, Nancy to Jo Binkley 1-8-1862
Demumbra, Rebecca F. to Jessee Boyd 12-23-1869 (12-24-1869)
Demumbra, Sarah C. to G. W. Boyd 6-26-1862
Demumbra, Sarah J. to John W. Simpkins 12-27-1869 (12-28-1869)
Denney, M. J. to John G. Fielder 1-6-1858
Denney, Virginia to James Williams 3-24-1869 (3-25-1869)
Denny, Catharine M. to G. W. Mullins 8-6-1866 (8-7-1866)
Denny, J. P. to Wm. L. Robertson 1-28-1858
Deuling?, M. J. to Edwin Taylor 3-19-1877 (3-21-1877)
Dill, Huldy H. to O. L. Teline 12-22-1868 (12-24-1868)
Dill, M. B. to B. H. Hatcher 1-21-1858
Dill, Martha A. to W. R. H. Jones 8-11-1875 (8-12-1875)
Dillingham, Letitia to L. J. Pack 5-4-1864
Dillingham, Lue F. to Wm. F. Osborn 2-14-1877
Dillingham, M. E. to J. D. Ham 5-29-1871 (6-1-1871)
Dillingham, M. E. to J. D. Sham 5-29-1871
Dillingham, Mattie E. to B. L. Pack 2-6-1879 (2-20-1879)
Dismukes, H. A. to John C. Black 1-16-1861 (1-17-1861)
Dismukes, Ida M. to G. W. Dyer 3-4-1880
Dismukes, M. C. to W. A. Williams 1-14-1865
Dismukes, P. W. to W. B. Kirkpatrick 4-15-1873 (4-16-1873)
Doolin, Sallie to Clay Adcock 3-19-1877
Douglas, Susan E. to Havy Page 11-28-1866
Douglass, Beesty? F. to W. M. Harris 12-18-1871 (12-19-1871)
Douglass, T. C. to J. W. Simpkins 7-10-1881
Douglass, Tona G. to George W. Stack 12-26-1872
Dow, Louisa H. to George L. Sloan 7-27-1858 (7-29-1858)
Dowlen, Carrie to J. A. Looney 10-4-1869
Dowlen, Huldah to W.F. Frey 10-15-1856
Dowlen, Lassa A. to William J. Hunt 8-14-1860 (8-16-1860)
Dowlen, M. A. to A. M. Copley 11-28-1871 (11-30-1871)
Dowlen, Mary Jane to John T. Newman 10-29-1870 (10-30-1870)
Dowlen, Mary T. to A. J. Perdue 1-11-1872
Dowling, M. T. to James H. Gupton 10-25-1860
Doyd?, Emma to Griffin Nicholson 7-3-1880 (7-4-1880)
Dozier, Elizabeth to Henry N. Kidd 12-28-1866 B
Dozier, Jane to G. W. McQuary? 4-10-1866 (4-11-1866)
Dozier, Judah A. to Leonedus Newsom 12-5-1870 (12-7-1870)
Dozier, Lutitia to A. C. Ragan 1-1-1873
Dozier, Margret A. to R. J. Hows 1-23-1869 (1-27-1869)
Dozier, Martha E. to F. H. Sllump 9-7-1859 (9-8-1859)
Dozier, Mary E. to C. C. McCall 8-14-1878 (8-15-1878)
Dozier, Mollie E. to A. W. Knight 9-27-1877
Dozier, Nancy to William Ussery 5-23-1864
Dozier, Nancy A. to Jessee Hooper 9-20-1861 (9-22-1861)
Dozier, Nancy I. to John B. Osborne 3-16-1867 (3-17-1867)
Dozier, Nancy J. to John B. Osborne 3-10-1867

Dozier, S. A. to David C. Hooper 8-27-1857
Drake, Elenor to J. P. Gardner 1-2-1860
Drake, Mary E. to Joseph D. Drake 4-15-1865
Drake?, Mary to George Washington 2-18-1881 (2-19-1881) B
Duncen, Lizzie to Lewis Kellum 4-4-1876 (4-7-1876) B
Dunlap, N. E. to G. Guin 1-5-1857
Dunn, Caroline R. to W. N. Thompson 9-18-1872
Dunn, Ellen to Luke Greer 1-19-1874 (1-25-1874) B
Dunn, Judith A. to A. B. Aken 1-13-1864
Dunn, L. J. to John A. Dean 5-28-1873 (5-29-1873)
Dunn, M. M. to William J. Gleason 3-30-1868 (4-7-1868)
Dunn, Margret M. to Moses G. Charlton 2-26-1878 (no return)
Dunn, Mary J. to Thos. W. Clark 11-26-1873 (11-27-1873)
Dunn, Rebecca J. to Wm. P. Mays 10-1-1860 (10-10-1860)
Durard, Eliza to James W. Morris 10-20-1866 (10-21-1866)
Durard, Elizabeth to Albert Darrow 4-24-1867 (4-25-1867)
Durham, Martha F. to J. T. Nicholson 9-2-1871 (9-5-1871)
Durham, Sarah B. to W. H. Farmer 11-5-1869
Dye, Laura to Edward M. Nolen 2-4-1861 (2-18-1861)
Dyer, Malinda to Edmond Dyer 7-27-1865 B
Easley, Anner to Wm. Thompson 3-1-1877 B
Easley, Sarah M. to Sam Brown 3-25-1875 B
Easley, Sayden to Robt. Brown 4-29-1877 (4-30-1877) B
Eastridge, Lucy to James H. Read 10-2-1869 (10-3-1869)
Eatherley, Nannie A. to J. T. Fielder 12-16-1878 (12-19-1878)
Eatherly, M. E. to H. W. Sanders 12-23-1857 (12-24-1857)
Eatherly, M. J. to J. T. Stewart 10-13-1877 (10-14-1877)
Eatherly, S. V. to G. W. Pinson 2-12-1870 (2-17-1870)
Eatherly, Sarah to Rufus Edwards 1-30-1863 (2-1-1863)
Eatherly, Tennessee to A. J. Simmons no date (with Feb 1867)
Edgin, Elizabeth to Alfred Jones 12-21-1861 (12-24-1861)
Edgin, Pracilla to John L. Richardson 10-17-1867
Edwards, Celary George Ann to Thomas Walker 12-29-1878
Edwards, D. A. to P. C. Williams 1-16-1860
Edwards, Dethed to Carril Walker 1-5-1866 B
Edwards, Emily to J.M. Wilson 3-19-1881 (3-20-1881) B
Edwards, George A. S. to Leander Walker 6-4-1868
Edwards, Mary J. to W. J. Stewart 12-28-1859
Edwards, Nancy A. T. to James M. Smith 11-8-1876 (11-10-1876)
Edwards, S. E. to W. A. Eatherly 1-21-1869 (1-28-1869)
Edwards, S. E. to D. A. Evans 12-21-1868 (12-22-1868)
Edwards, V. E. to W. E. Edwards 1-3-1876
Edwards?, Susan to James Young 3-15-1865
Elliott, Chairity M. to H. E. Crawford 11-22-1866
Elliott, Susan to Robt. Pennington 12-31-1861
Ellis, Minnie S. to W. S. Jarnnett 10-25-1878 (10-27-1878)
Erls, Martha F. to Daniel W. Turner 12-22-1870
Evans, Mary to Mason Perdue 12-25-1871 (12-28-1871) B
Everett, Lou to Wm. Williams 1-2-1874 B
Everett, Martha to A. P. Hiland 11-22-1866
Everette, F. to A. J. Hudgens 4-3-1861 (4-7-1861)
Ewing, Sallie to Jerry Hooper 7-29-1873
Exum, S. B. C. to J. H. Judd 6-19-1869 (6-20-1869)
Farlen, Susan to David Watkins 10-30-1875 (10-21?-1876?) B

Farmbrough, Mossa to Robert Farmbrugh 4-16-1857
Farmer, Caroline to Elijah Woodson 4-16-1869 (4-17-1869) B
Farmer, Eliza to Johnerthan Green 3-15-1869 (3-16-1869)
Farmer, Elizabeth to Wm. Oliver 12-25-1871
Farmer, Emma to Bailie P. Jones 3-28-1874
Farmer, Harriet to H. C. Cates 11-23-1875
Farmer, Josephine to John Bennett 2-22-1877 (2-23-1877)
Farmer, Martha Ann to William Rase 8-13-1879 (8-14-1879)
Felts, A. H. to W. F. Frey 1-10-1874 (1-13-1874)
Felts, Ann E. to James H. Mayo 9-29-1873 (10-1-1873)
Felts, Anna R. to James D. Hicks 10-10-1867
Felts, Celia to Aaron Williams 7-4-1866 B
Felts, Elizabeth to George Anderson 10-10-1866 (10-11-1866)
Felts, Frances to James Nichols 6-26-1869 (6-27-1869)
Felts, Laticia to J. W. Carney 9-11-1869
Felts, Martha to John R. Procter 1-4-1871
Felts, Martha F. to Geo. W. Binkley 6-29-1864
Felts, Martha P. to W. H. Morris 2-15-1860 (2-16-1860)
Felts, Mary to Wilie Woodall 7-17-1872 (7-18-1872)
Felts, Mary D. to William R. Ramer 10-11-1865
Felts, Mary J. to Robert Fleaney 1-23-1877 (1-24-1877)
Felts, N. J. to D. C. Council 1-23-1871 (1-25-1871)
Felts, Nancy to M. Binkley 10-15-1866 (10-17-1866)
Felts, Roena to J. L. Girard 8-6-1872 (8-7-1872)
Felts, S. J. to J. H. Carney 1-20-1881
Felts, S. J. to Joshua Carney 2-15-1877
Felts, Sarah E. to T. D. Council 1-7-1867 (1-9-1867)
Felts, Susan to E. B. Carney 2-1-1865
Felts, Susan R. to Daid C. Cullum 8-21-1867
Felts, Virgina D. to Andrew K. Douglas 10-18-1878 (10-19-1878)
Ferebee, Meriah to John Shelton 2-28-1871 B
Ferrell, E. R. to W. W. Warner 10-4-1858
Ferrile, Elizabeth to Jordan Hooper 5-24-1856
Fetts, Eliz. H. to John Shivers 2-11-1857
Fetts, F. H. to G. B. Harris 10-21-1858
Fetts, Marina to Wm. L. Brinkley 11-14-1857 (11-15-1857)
Fetts, Mary to A. J. Perdue 8-30-1859
Fetts, Rosa to William Casey 11-21-1862
Fielder, Loucinda to John T. Gibbs 1-30-1879
Fielder, Mary A. to William Denney 7-19-1862 (7-24-1862)
Finch, S. to S. Brown 2-12-1881 (2-14-1881)
Flenen, Briley to Isaac Keith 8-1-1880
Fletcher, Eliza to James Garland 7-23-1867 (7-24-1867)
Flintoff, E. W. to Z. Shearon 10-6-1863 (10-7-1863)
Ford, Angeline to James Farmer 7-4-1866
Ford, Marth A. to Joseph Maberry 2-17-1857 (2-18-1857)
Ford, Martha A. to C. F. Allen 7-11-1870
Ford, Nancy to Samuel H. Haggard 11-14-1866 (11-15-1866)
Ford, Sarah to Lewis H. Wilson 6-22-1867 (6-28-1867)
Forehand, C. A. to William Mayfield 1-6-1863 (1-8-1863)
Fortane, Louisa J. to William Dowlen 12-24-1861
Fortune, S. E. to Henry Dowlen 2-21-1866
Foster, Sarah to Lenard Binkley 3-25-1864
Fox, Jane E. to Thos. A. Owen 12-13-1869 (12-16-1869)

Fox, Mary L. to J. D. Vanhook 1-26-1861 (1-27-1861)
Fraley, Mildred to S. H. Demumbra 12-22-1877 (12-23-1877)
Frazier, Emily to W. P. Nicholson 10-25-1879 (10-26-1879)
Frazier, Geriline to John Gupton 11-3-1879 (11-6-1879)
Frazier, M. E. to Z. Shearon 10-16-1876 (10-19-1876)
Frazier, M. E. to M. G. Twiner 10-27-1880 (10-28-1880)
Frazier, M. S. to S. H. Becker? 3-6-1875 (3-7-1875)
Frazier, Mary to Evans Bass 1-11-1871 B
Frazier, Mary T. to G. W. Kelly 12-14-1867 (12-16-1867)
Frazier, Netta to J. W. Fielder 2-5-1877 (2-8-1877)
Frey, Emer to H. M. Clinard 6-3-1879 (6-5-1879)
Frey, M. T. to T. S. Teasley 10-15-1873 (10-16-1873)
Frey, Mary to G. W. Basford 9-6-1875 (9-8-1875)
Fry, Beattrice to J. B. Hyde 11-27-1878 (11-28-1878)
Fulgham, B. B. to R. J. Mayes 3-11-1877
Fulgham, H. R. to N. P. Sneed 1-14-1867 (1-15-1867)
Fulgham, M. C. to W. J. Fulghum 8-7-1876 (8-16-1876)
Fulghum, Lucada to S. K. Dann 5-11-1865 (5-18-1865)
Fulghum, M. E. to R. W. Pegram 9-17-1861 (9-25-1861)
Fulghum, Rebecca B. to J. B. Thompson 5-11-1865 (5-18-1865)
Fulghum, Sallie P. to Austin O. Lynn 7-11-1864 (7-14-1864)
Fulghum, Sallie W. to Green Wood Payne 6-3-1869
Fulghum, Virginia A. to M. L. Moore 7-11-1864 (7-14-1864)
Fults, George Ann to John Patton 12-22-1877 (12-23-1877)
Funch, Elizabeth to Jessie W. Ham 12-13-1873 (12-18-1873)
Gallaher, Ellen D. to William M. Pegram 2-20-1864
Gallaher, I. J. to W. C. jr. Hutton 2-2-1872 (2-7-1872)
Gallaher, L. A. to James Pegram 9-5-1868
Gardner, E. C. to W. J. Darden 11-10-1866
Garland, S. P. to M. V. Pack 1-27-1877 (1-28-1877)
Gatewood, Charlotte V. to Augustin Anderson 8-15-1880
Gerdrick, Margaret to Curtis Bush 8-1-1878 (8-4-1878) B
Gibbs, Emily M. to G. W. Binkley 6-14-1862
Gibbs, Fannie to Simion Morris 3-5-1878 (3-6-1878)
Gibbs, M. E. to A. J. Crantz 3-23-1867 (3-27-1867)
Gibbs, Margret J. to Wm. H. Obrian 10-4-1869 (10-5-1869)
Gibbs, Martha W. to Joseph Morris 1-30-1868
Gibbs, Susan to W. b. Blankinship 3-5-1878 (3-6-1878)
Gillam, Elizabeth to James P. Shadrick 3-17-1868
Glasscock, Mary Adline to Andrew Butterfield 12-30-1878
Gleaves, Lizzie M. to J. W. Simpkins 4-25-1876
Gleeves, M. L. to R. J. Felts 6-28-1880
Goddard, Cytha P. to Thos. J. Binkley 12-23-1868
Godsey, Nancy E. to B. C. Dillingham 7-29-1857
Gorden, Amanda to Colman Ussery 3-19-1873 B
Gossett, Virginia T. to James T. Wilson 11-11-1868 (11-13-1868)
Gower, Sis? to W. J. Edward 10-22-1878 (10-31-1878)
Gower, T. E. to James Davis 1-12-1858 (1-13-1858)
Gray, Dicy to George Dunn 3-22-1874 (3-26-1874) B
Gray, Mary Jane to Enoch Reed 3-15-1881
Gray, R. J. to William Walker 11-25-1858 (12-1-1858)
Gray, Savanah T. to J. S. McGhee 10-29-1872 (11-10-1872)
Gray, T. A. N. to W. L. Marwarning 5-29-1858 (5-30-1858)
Gray, V. L. to G. F. Gower 1-7-1871 (1-11-1871)

Green, Mary A. to Green Allen 12-14-1860
Greene, A. T. to Aaron Lipe 4-12-1871 (4-13-1871)
Greene, Alvy J. to St. Leger Scott 1-19-1871
Greene, S. A. to James Speight 2-27-1867
Greene, Susan E. to James R. Douglas 5-19-1860 (5-20-1860)
Greer, Elizabeth to Mark Garton 1-6-1857 (1-7-1857)
Greer, Mary to George Kellum 5-14-1870 (5-21-1870) B
Greer, Mary to William Yates 2-6-1862
Greer, Priscilla to Joseph Yates 1-16-1875 (1-21-1875)
Griffin, Mollie A. to J. F. Sullivean 10-10-1879
Griggsby, E. J. to Green Worthey 3-4-1863
Grigsby, E. J. to Green Worthy 3-4-1863
Grine, M. F. to C. D. Grimes 11-27-1876
Grove, E. F. to J.L. Claxton 9-28-1871
Grown, Jemima to D. W. Hooper 12-1-1866 (12-9-1866)
Gupton, Eliza to L. F. Smith 2-4-1878 (2-6-1878)
Gupton, Henrietta to J. W. Gupton 10-28-1873 (10-29-1873)
Gupton, Henrietta L. to John M. Duke 3-8-1869
Gupton, Lucy Jane to G. H. Frazier 1-7-1880
Gupton, M. P. to J. W. Maberry 12-27-1873 (1-1-1874)
Gupton, Martha J. to John J. Gupton 5-9-1871 (5-10-1871)
Gupton, Mary A. to John M. Smith 4-15-1859
Gupton, Mary B. to Wm. Jones 12-20-1875
Gupton, Mattie A. to Allen J. Harrison 9-13-1861
Gupton, Sarah P. to J. H. W. Hunt 1-23-1872
Gupton, Sarah T. to A. S. Blankenship 11-21-1868 (11-22-1868)
Guptono, Sarah Elizabeth to John Tyson 4-22-1879 (4-23-1879)
Hagewood, Amy to Jackson Menroe 12-15-1876 (12-21-1876)
Hagewood, Cerdely A. to J. A. Hagewood 8-4-1876 (8-27-1876)
Hagewood, Dora to J. M. Procter 10-9-1876 (10-13-1876)
Hagewood, Lyddia to W. Hagewood 4-15-1878 (no return)
Hagewood, Mary D. to J. W. D. Hagewood 10-6-1879 (10-30-1879)
Haggerd, Allice to M. M. Knox 11-18-1876 (11-19-1876)
Haguewood, Dolla to John Higgins 4-7-1879 (4-16-1879)
Hagwewood, Fredonia to H. M. Maberry 2-18-1873
Hagwood, M. P. to W. H. Daniel 12-15-1860 (12-16-1860)
Hagwood, S. L. to J. H. Batson 9-10-1879 (9-11-1879)
Hain, Sarah Jane to John N. Dillingham 2-9-1871 (2-23-1871)
Hain?, Clarasy to Robert Thompson 1-28-1869 (1-29-1869) B
Hale, A. T. to T. J. Adkisson 1-10-1866
Hale, J. S. to A. F. Allen 5-11-1872 (5-12-1872)
Hale, Lucada to W. J. Crouch 9-21-1861 (9-22-1861)
Hale, Maggie to A. J. Colvin 10-6-1873 (10-9-1873)
Hale, Mariah to Richard Slodge 10-11-1873 (10-12-1873) B
Hale, Mary E. to L. A. Rhea 9-9-1876 (9-10-1876)
Hale, Mattie to Moses McCrea 1-22-1876   B
Hale, N. L. to S. L. Jones 12-4-1877 (12-9-1877)
Hale, Priscilla to James Hooper 4-25-1878 (4-28-1878)
Hall, Elizabeth E. to C. J. Richardson 3-26-1864 (3-27-1864)
Hall, Mary Ann to John Praw? 3-9-1868 (3-10-1868)
Hall, Narcissa to Pike Everett 9-24-1868
Halstead, Harriet to Zackariah Jones 12-25-1875 (12-26-1875)
Halstead, Virginia A. to Thos. R. Laughlin 1-23-1869 (2-3-1869)
Ham, Margaret L. to David A. Eakin 12-16-1875 (12-23-1875)

Ham, Mary E. to William Carrel 12-30-1867 (12-31-1867)
Hamble, Maggie A. to Roger J. Maney? 12-26-1876 (12-27-1876)
Hambrick, Sarah E. to S. J. Garland 12-30-1875
Hamlet, Mary J. to W. W. Morison 6-9-1858
Hampton, M.J. to W. T. Adkisson 2-19-1861 (2-20-1861)
Hampton, Mary to Ed Walker 3-2-1879 B
Hampton, Mary to Ed Walker 3-2-1879 B
Hampton, Nancy M. to J. P. Mosier 11-27-1873
Hand, Gracy to Aaron Collins 5-25-1867 (5-26-1867) B
Hannah, Amanda to James P. Clark 7-29-1859 (8-3-1859)
Hannah, Caty to Cezar Greer 2-16-1871 B
Hannah, Gennie to John Swiney? 9-21-1877 (9-22-1877) B
Hannah, Mary to Jarmin Ussery 12-23-1874 B
Harding, Floria to Giddy Hudgens 1-15-1880 B
Harding, M. J. to F. W. Williams 7-8-1865
Harper, Elizabeth to Alexander Teasley 4-11-1868 (4-12-1868)
Harper, Mary to A. F. Carney 6-29-1859
Harper, Mary J. to R. J. Johnson 5-3-1873
Harper, Medora to Washington Gray 3-20-1880 (3-21-1880)
Harper, Narcissa O. to J. F. Smith 2-18-1873 (2-23-1873)
Harper, Sarah to Jessee Shearon 12-16-1862
Harper, Tennessee to John M. Teasly 12-6-1870 (12-7-1870)
Harrenton, Jane to Sampson Perry 11-29-1871 (11-30-1871)
Harrington, Elizabeth to H. Tomlin 6-30-1877 (6-31?-1877)
Harrington, July to J. W. Mays 3-17-1881
Harrington, Mary H. to G. W. Harrington 10-20-1858 (10-21-1858)
Harrington, U.? to A. J. Ventress 3-10-1859 (3-30-1859)
Harris, Alice L. to Charles M. Cooley 7-24-1874 (7-26-1874)
Harris, Amelia to J. Z. Hudgens 9-25-1856
Harris, Amelia A. to John H. Teasley 9-30-1872 (10-3-1872)
Harris, Ann E. to Thos. J. Dozier 10-5-1872
Harris, Delvira George Ann to Thomas Walker (no dates)
Harris, Elizabeth to Hosa Satterfield 9-14-1868 (9-15-1868)
Harris, Elizabeth W. to J. J. Nicholson 2-2-1869
Harris, G. A. to J. B. Johnson 7-3-1876 (7-4-1876)
Harris, George Ann to John Montgomery 12-16-1878   B
Harris, Harriet to Thos. J. Williams 4-5-1869
Harris, Kissie to A. J. Binkley 2-28-1865
Harris, L. Y.? to Henry Hunt 12-18-1880 (12-23-1880) B
Harris, Lucinda to S. C. Harris 3-25-1861 (3-28-1861)
Harris, Ludry? G. to John H. Clark 12-13-1876
Harris, Luvenia to Rufus Harris 12-28-1871 (12-29-1871)
Harris, M. R. to B. J. Corlew 10-30-1878
Harris, Margret to Wm. J. Hale 9-28-1869 (10-3-1869)
Harris, Margret to A. L. Hudgens 10-19-1869 (10-23-1869)
Harris, Martha to R. W. Felts 7-27-1864
Harris, Martha to William Frey? 7-4-1867 (7-7-1867) B
Harris, Martha E. to John N. Laughran 9-2-1869 (9-5-1869)
Harris, Mary A. to John Bell 12-22-1866 (12-25-1866) B
Harris, Mary M. to D. A. Reed 4-18-1879 (4-20-1879)
Harris, Nancy to Z. F. Shearon 9-1-1865
Harris, Rebecca Jane to G. W. Teasley 9-18-1878 (9-19-1878)
Harris, S. D. to H. J. Carney 9-6-1860
Harris, Sarah to W. H. Plasters 1-8-1868 (1-9-1868)

Harris, Sarah to A. D. Smith 10-5-1874 (10-8-1874)
Harris, Sarah E. to W. J. Read 7-22-1876
Harris, Tennessee to Andrew Robertson 12-24-1866 (12-26-1866) B
Harrison, Martha (Mrs.) to W. H. Brinkley 11-7-1871 (11-9-1871)
Hatcher, Eliza F. to N. B. Phipps 12-12-1860 (12-17-1860)
Hatcher, Lucy J. to B. F. Smith 1-18-1859 (1-19-1859)
Hatfield, Olive W. to Joseph Carter 11-20-1878   B
Hatfield, Ollie W. to Joseph Carter 11-30-1878 (no return)
Hays?, Mollie to Henry Parkerson 4-8-1876   B
Haywood, Martha E. to Thomas H. Rye 5-2-1859
Hazan, Caroline to James Scott 7-28-1870 (7-30-1870) B
Head, Drebra to W. R. Harris 4-30-1872 (5-2-1872)
Head, Fanny to John Batson 1-28-1871   B
Head, Louisa to David Mallory 12-26-1877 (12-27-1877) B
Hefner, Nancy C. F. to George B. Hasley 9-1-1865
Helton, Nannie G. to Wm. C. Greer 7-24-1877 (7-25-1877)
Henderson, E. B. to Thos. T. Osborne 1-9-1858
Henderson, M. J. to William L. Cullum 3-6-1857 (3-15-1857)
Henderson, Margret E. to Wm. R. Felts 12-24-1870 (12-25-1870)
Henderson, Mary A. to Nathan Morris 1-23-1862
Henderson, Mary R. to J. B. Williams 10-18-1880 (10-21-1880)
Henderson, Susan M. to Alex. E. Boyte 4-5-1879 (4-6-1879)
Henry, Harriett E. to Nathan G. B. Greer 1-31-1881 (2-3-1881)
Henry, Margret to Genrl. J. Greer 2-8-1870
Henry, Sallie A. to H. A. Herrin 7-10-1876 (7-16-1876)
Herrin, Alice E. to Elenso D. Liles 12-4-1875 (12-16-1875)
Herrin, Eugenia to Miles D. Spencer 6-2-1877 (6-3-1877)
Hesbey?, Nancy to George Head 4-21-1881   B
Hicks, Caroline to W. J. Cox 4-24-1878
Higgins, Sarah M. F. to Hiram B. Baker 8-26-1867 (8-29-1867)
Highland, Alice to S. W. Long 4-27-1881 (5-1-1881)
Hitower, Eliza to Joseph Lenox 3-20-1869 (3-24-1869) B
Hogue, Emaline to S. W. Thomson 8-23-1864
Hollis, E. J. to I. W. Simmons 11-4-1875
Hollis, J. J. to J. B. Allen 1-17-1878 (no return)
Hollis, Martha L. to Y. J. Hampton 2-28-1878 (3-1-1878)
Hollis, Melissa A. to J. B. Cain 10-22-1870
Holmes, Elizabeth to William Bright 9-6-1861
Holmes, Martha to James L. Bright 2-20-1862
Holt, Martha to David Beck 4-14-1871   B
Hooper, A. J. to A. P. jr. Dozier 12-20-1880 (12-21-1880)
Hooper, A. P. to W. J. Reggan 11-29-1878 (12-1-1878)
Hooper, Alice to Edwin Harris 11-30-1877 (12-2-1877) B
Hooper, Alice to Charles Teasley 6-19-1880 (6-20-1880) B
Hooper, Alice V. to A. A. Mathews 11-10-1880
Hooper, Amanda to B. S. Miles 12-10-1856 (12-11-1856)
Hooper, Bell to G. L. Lovell 11-17-1877 (11-22-1877)
Hooper, Ellen A. to William Jackson 1-13-1869 (1-14-1869)
Hooper, Fredonia A. to James E. Bradley 2-7-1861
Hooper, Jenne to J. W. Dozier 10-25-1862 (10-29-1862)
Hooper, Josephine to S. B. Alley 5-1-1869 (5-2-1869)
Hooper, L. to Clarence Watson 10-13-1867 (10-20-1867) B
Hooper, Laura A. to John H. Lovell 1-25-1876 (1-26-1876)
Hooper, M. C. to John C. Hale 6-5-1858 (6-6-1858)

Hooper, M. R. to Sam Kirkpatrick 2-12-1867? (2-13-1861)
Hooper, Martha to J. W. Williams 6-13-1874 (6-14-1874)
Hooper, Mary to James L. Russell 1-17-1866
Hooper, Mary E. G. to Robert S. Obrien 11-29-1871
Hooper, Mary? E. to T. A. Woodson 12-29-1870 (1-3-1871)
Hooper, Mehala to John Pane 9-24-1856 (9-25-1856)
Hooper, Mollie to Charles Lewis 2-17-1877 (2-27-1877) B
Hooper, N. E. to L. H. Cullum 2-21-1867 (2-22-1867)
Hooper, Nancy D.? to M. V. Hicks 1-1-1869
Hooper, Nancy T. to William B. Nichols 1-10-1857
Hooper, Phoebe J. to G. A. Scott 1-20-1881
Hooper, S. A. to J. H. Biggin 11-22-1856
Hooper, Sarah D. to A. G. Goodlett 9-6-1863
Hooper, Susan E. to P. H. Dozier 10-8-1872 (10-9-1872)
Hooper, Thursa C. to W. C. C. Nichol 12-18-1861 (12-22-1861)
Hooper, Una to Robert L. Nichol 8-15-1864
Hooper, Virgina to Joseph Krantz 7-18-1868 (7-19-1868)
Huddleston, Clen? to Jerre Woodmore? 2-7-1880 (3-28-1880) B
Hudelston, Harriet to Alfred Greer 4-1-1878 B
Hudgens, America to Morris Hudgens 12-10-1874 (12-13-1874) B
Hudgens, Arminty to Joshua Edwards 3-25-1870 B
Hudgens, C. J. to S. Dowlen 1-15-1870 (1-20-1870)
Hudgens, E. C. to W. W. Read 10-27-1860 (11-18-1860)
Hudgens, Elizabeth to William Davis 6-1-1874 (6-2-1874)
Hudgens, Ellen Lee to Frank Albritton 3-24-1880
Hudgens, Fanny to William Hyde 12-27-1866 (12-28-1866) B
Hudgens, Harriet to Samuel Balthrop 9-21-1872 (9-22-1872) B
Hudgens, J. T. to W. L. Bradley 7-5-1858 (7-8-1858)
Hudgens, Jennie to E. L. Lee 11-16-1876 B
Hudgens, Josephine to Jessee Aker? 12-22-1879 B
Hudgens, Lucian to Thos. H. Perry 1-10-1876 (1-12-1876)
Hudgens, Lucy A. to Wesley Edwards 11-15-1876 (11-18-1876) B
Hudgens, Mary to L. E. Hunt 2-21-1862 (3-6-1862)
Hudgens, Mary to Lewis H. Justice 12-27-1879 (12-28-1879) B
Hudgens, N. G. to J. H. Simmons 9-26-1878 (9-29-1878)
Hudgens, Nancy to Wm. E. Teasley 12-11-1869 (12-13-1869)
Hudgeons, Josephine to York Hudgens 1-6-1870 (1-7-1870) B
Huggins, Josaphine to J. L. Rosson 1-22-1879 (1-23-1879)
Humphreys, C. to Wm. R. Pool 12-24-1857
Humphreys, Lydia to Simon Hunt 9-14-1867 (9-15-1867) B
Humphreys, Mary to Richard Nichols 5-10-1872 (5-11-1872) B
Hunt, Alice E. N. to Wm. R. Vick 1-23-1879
Hunt, Anna to George Major 2-1-1873 B
Hunt, Elizabeth to G. M. Smith 10-14-1878 (10-15-1878)
Hunt, Fannie to Sim Bryant 6-24-1871 B
Hunt, Margret L. to H. J. Binkley 4-17-1858
Hunt, Mary E. to D. C. Cullum 12-14-1859 (12-29-1860?)
Hunt, Mary E. to R. F. Nicholson 12-25-1878
Hunt, Melissa to Alert Walker 4-13-1878 (4-14-1878) B
Hunt, P.? C. to C. A. Wilkins 12-2-1867 (12-11?-1867)
Hunt, Victoria to Colemon Nicholson 12-28-1872 (12-29-1872)
Hunt, Zepharin O. M. to W. T. Maxey 12-28-1869
Hunter, Elizabeth to George Rudolph 3-30-1880 (3-31-1880)
Hunter, Emer L. to G. W. Smith 3-4-1878 (3-6-1878)

Hunter, Geraline to Benj. Williams 12-28-1867 (7-11-1868) B
Hunter, L. A. to William Frazier 11-15-1865
Hunter, M. A. to W. T. Gossett 1-4-1859 (1-6-1859)
Hunter, M. E. to J. H. Batts 12-16-1879
Hunter, Martha P. to J. O. Smith 2-23-1875 (2-25-1875)
Hunter, Mary E. to Thos. T. Balthrop 12-11-1868 (12-15-1868)
Hunter, Mary J. to Alex Humphrey 2-5-1874 B
Hunter, Metilda to Lewey Nichol 4-26-1867 (4-27-1867) B
Hunter, Sallie to Peter Williams 4-17-1876 (4-20-1876) B
Hutton, Mary Ann to Walter J. Kline 6-18-1872
Hutton, Susan to Shadrick Kellum 5-11-1870 (5-13-1870) B
Hyde, Amanda to Joseph Nicholson 9-4-1880 (9-5-1880) B
Hyde, Callinhite? to James Speight 3-15-1879 (3-16-1879) B
Hyde, Lucinda to Wm. Henry Hudgens 1-30-1873 (2-2-1873) B
Hyde, Penola to W. H. Chambliss 12-22-1873 (12-23-1873)
Ingle, Lou to D. N. Nye 1-7-1874 (1-15-1874)
Inman, E. A. to R. W. Brian 9-10-1867 (9-12-1867)
Innman, L. E. to F. P. Head 11-3-1873
Ivy, Mary to Thomas Dickins? 2-5-1867 (2-6-1867)
Jackson, D. A. to C. C. Jackson 9-18-1867 B
Jackson, Delila to Andrew Robertson 9-6-1872 (9-7-1872) B
Jackson, Esther Ann R. to J. R. Williams 10-5-1872 (10-6-1872)
Jackson, Lou to Samel Woodmoore 7-26-1875 (7-27-1874?) B
Jackson, Lucy to Wyatt Bryant 7-19-1856 (7-25-1856)
Jackson, Margret A. to Geo. W. Shaver 12-13-1869
Jackson, Martha J. to Wm. H. Whitworth 6-21-1866 (6-25-1866)
Jackson, Nancy J. to John Basford 11-22-1866
Jackson, Susan to Peter Mosley 3-20-1869 (3-21-1869) B
Jarrel, Sarah to John T. Dwiss? 6-2-1863
Jenett, Arlena to John Y. Henderson 12-19-1856 (12-17?-1856)
Jenkins, Emma to Jos. Gatewood 12-3-1880 (12-5-1880)
Jenkins, Ida to Maro Woodson 1-26-1881 (1-27-1881)
Jenkins, Mary to J. N. Shearon 1-5-1874
Jennett, E. A. to W. B. Ransdale 12-4-1858
Jennett, Mary A. to W. A. Swift 10-12-1859 (10-13-1859)
Jennett, Sarah A. to Z. W. Owen 11-18-1872 (11-19-1872)
Jent, Sally Ann to J. W. True 5-15-1862
Johns, Faney to James McCormic 6-22-1866 (6-25-1866)
Johnson, Catharine to Davy Newsom 8-24-1875 B
Johnson, Elizabeth to Johnathan Hollis 9-24-1872
Johnson, Indiana to A. P. Hiland 9-3-1877 (8?-5-1877)
Johnson, M. R. to Thos. C. Jones 3-20-1860
Johnson, Mersie to N. B. Harris 12-12-1873 (12-14-1873)
Johnson, Sarah to James W. Marall 10-22-1874
Jones, Fannie to Wm. Carrol 3-3-1879 (3-6-1879)
Jones, Judy A. to G. W. C. C. Major 9-26-1861
Jones, Mamma to Ellis _____ 1-2-1867 (1-13-1867) B
Jones, Marana V. to Amos R. Wilson 9-24-1866 (9-27-1866)
Jones, Marth E. to James W. Fields 6-9-1862 (6-12-1862)
Jones, Martha to Franklin Gupton 3-8-1881 (3-9-1881)
Jones, Martha to B. B. Hale 2-26-1877 (2-28-1877)
Jones, Martha to Olliver Ross 10-24-1873 B
Jones, Mary A. to Edmond Collins 4-13-1866 (4-14-1866) B
Jones, Mary C. to James D. Matthews 12-7-1871 (12-14-1871)

Jones, Mary E. to James W. Greer 12-16-1867 (12-19-1867)
Jones, Miley to Joshua Collins 9-25-1873 B
Jones, Moaning? to W. H. Miles 1-13-1877 (1-18-1877)
Jones, Nancy E. to Andrew J. Crall 9-25-1857
Jones, P. A. F. to James Hunter 4-8-1858 (4-9-1858)
Jordan, A. E. to S. W. Cox 7-30-1864
Jordan, Elizabeth to Ehud? Gower 7-10-1866
Jordan, Lizzie to A. J. Crouch 12-5-1874
Jordan, Lucada F. to John N. Allen 4-15-1876 (4-16-1876)
Jordan, Nancy to Thomas E. Cox 8-22-1861
Jordan, Polly to George Mumford 4-3-1869 (4-6-1869) B
Jordan, Rebecca to Thomas J. Crouch 6-28-1859
Jordan, S. E. to R. G. Lovell 10-14-1874 (10-15-1874)
Jordan, Samuel Ellen to F. M. Hooper 10-13-1874
Jordan, Sarah S. to R. W. Price 1-2-1875 (1-3-1875)
Jordan, Susan to Shadrick Farley 11-19-1866 B
Justice, Emily to J. T. Walls 2-28-1878
Justice, Mary E. to Jas. H. Majors 11-5-1857
Keeler, Eliza Ann to W. L. Morris 10-23-1869 (10-24-1869)
Keeler, Mary to C. R. Felts 12-20-1875 (12-22-1875)
Keeler, Sarah J. to W. C. Roach 9-14-1871 (9-17-1871)
Kellum, Elenor to Newsom B. Mays 11-24-1858
Kellum, Isabella to E. G. Sears 5-30-1870 (6-1-1870)
Kerby, Mary E. to A. J. Dozier 7-22-1876 (7-23-1876)
Kinchlow?, Tennessee to William Russell 7-23-1874
King, Eliz. to F. Grimes 12-31-1857
King, Ida A. to T. B. Frazier 12-19-1879 (12-21-1879)
King, Sarah to N. McCormack 4-27-1861 (4-28-1861)
Kistley, Anne to G. W. Neighbors 7-28-1880 (7-29-1880)
Knight, Dicy Jane to Andrew Arcly? 11-18-1868 (11-19-1868)
Knight, Frances T. to James Harrington 2-5-1878
Knight, George Ann to Robt. Clinard 1-9-1877
Knight, Harrett A. to Geo. M. Allen 7-3-1880
Knight, Josephine to John Baxter 8-3-1874
Knight, Julia to Henry Mays 5-28-1877 B
Knight, Lethy B. to William H. Mathews 11-26-1868
Knight, Mary to Joseph Mosier 11-1-1858 (11-3-1858)
Knight, Nancy to E. J. Clark no date (with Jul 1865)
Knight, Sarah to R. Chambless 10-30-1861
Knight, Sarah A. to George Dowlen 7-14-1862
Knight, Sary to Willie C. Cantrel 4-15-1881
Knight, Tennessee to Cheatham Ramer 4-22-1880
Knox, Henretta to Zack Jennett 4-15-1873 (4-17-1873)
Knox, Lucy A. to Frank Jennett 1-13-1868 (1-16-1868)
Knox, Mary Jane to J. D. Rossen 4-22-1876 (4-27-1876)
Knox, Nancy J. to G. F. Ellis 12-27-1866 (12-31-1866)
Knox, Sarah to John Harris 4-14-1879 (4-17-1879)
Knox, V. B. to S. N. Clifton 4-18-1866
Krantz, Everlin to M. C. Newman 2-23-1881 (2-24-1881)
Krantz, Everline to George W. Beele 8-18-1879
Krantz, M. J. to J. W. Sanders 3-31-1870
Krantz, Martha F. to James A. Rose 12-2-1876
Krantz, Mary A. to B. F. Read 5-6-1868 (5-7-1868)
Krantz, Mary M. S. to F. P. Binkley 9-14-1874 (9-20-1874)

Krantz, Rose Ann to A. W. Sample 7-3-1868 (7-5-1868)
Krantz, Tilda J. to B. C. Richardson 5-13-1870
Kreider, G. V. H. to W. W. Kellum 9-17-1861 (9-19-1861)
Lanier, A. E. to James R. Walker 4-23-1873
Lanier, Rosa C. to Joel J. Harris 8-5-1868 (8-6-1868)
Lankford, Fannie to Clay Weakley 6-22-1881 (6-23-1881) B
Lawrence, M. E. to E. S. Ellis 5-26-1877 (5-27-1877)
Lay, Lougenia to Amos Marcus Harris 12-13-1878 (12-15-1878)
Lee, Anna to Joseph Lyles 3-12-1874   B
Lee, Emily to Robert White 8-14-1873   B
Lee, Julia F. to Samuel H. Dunn 12-13-1859
Lee, Julia F. to Samuel H. Dunn 12-13-1859 (12-29-1859)
Lee, Minty to John Bell 6-11-1856
Leigh, Amer E. to Tuck? Sterry 12-29-1880 (12-30-1880)
Lenox, Lucy to W. C. Walker 2-7-1880 (2-8-1880) B
Lenox, M. A. to W. P. Lawrence 9-25-1880 (9-26-1880)
Lenox, Mary Y. to Jessee T. Edwards 11-6-1866 (11-13-1866)
Lenox, Sarah J. to T. C. Cato 12-10-1864
Lenox, Tennie A. to Hiram B. Carney 11-20-1860
Lewis, C. M. to W. L. Morris 7-26-1858 (8-1-1858)
Lewis, Charlott M. to E. B. Cerney 8-18-1856 (9-25-1856)
Lewis, S. to E. Simmons 6-21-1858 (7-4-1858)
Lightfoot, Larry to Edwin Coffee no date (with 1865) B
Liles, Buthinda M. J. to Calvin Abshere 7-11-1868 (7-22-1868)
Link, Margia J. to B. M. Jordon 2-15-1881 (2-17-1881)
Litle, Jane to Larkin Harrington 4-11-1870
Logan, Mary Ann to Robt. McCormack 11-25-1876 (11-26-1876)
Long, Bridget to Cornelius O. Laughlin 2-11-1860 (4-22-1860)
Lovell, Catharine to Andrew Hoge 10-9-1862 (10-15-1862)
Lovell, E. K. to A. J. Newsom 1-3-1866 (1-4-1866)
Lovell, E. L. to W. J. Hooper 12-16-1859 (12-21-1859)
Lovell, Elizabeth to F. M. Hooper 12-8-1874 (12-9-1874)
Lovell, Emiline to P. C. Thomson 10-15-1864
Lovell, Irene to Thomas H. Cullum 11-18-1869
Lovell, L. to M. V. B. Hicks 2-23-1861 (2-24-1861)
Lovell, Louisanna to A. C. Watkins 12-27-1859 (1-1-1860)
Lovell, Mary to W. S. Crouch 12-24-1874 (12-28-1874)
Lovell, Mollie to G. F. Cullun 12-30-1874
Lovell, Nancy to S. H. Hows 2-13-1867 (2-14-1867)
Lovell, Nanny to Wm. C. Hoobury 10-10-1874 (10-6?-1874)
Lovell, P. M. to W. A. Cothren 8-22-1861
Lovell, Patsey M. to W. A. Cothren 8-22-1861
Lovell, Rebecca P. to __. Williams 10-27-1859
Lovell, S. T. to W. N. Dozier 1-10-1865
Lowe, Anna M. to W. P. Lovejoy 11-22-1871
Lowe, Louisa to W. D. Gleaves 1-2-1860 (1-4-1860)
Lowe, Sallie D. to J. M. Viverett 2-20-1879
Lowe, Sarah E. to M. Thomas 1-30-1866
Mackbee, Susan H. to William J. Miller 12-19-1860 (12-20-1860)
Major, Emily to Clinton Jo___ 5-17-1880 (5-18-1880)
Major, Emily to Clinton Jones 5-17-1880 (5-18-1880)
Major, Penelope to D. C. Perdue 8-19-1867 (8-20-1867)
Major, Sarah A. to James B Kelley 8-31-1868 (8?-2-1868)
Majors, Ann to Aleck Shaw 12-27-1869 (12-28-1869) B

Majors, E. to W. M. Stewart 2-2-1866
Majors, Eliz. to Robert D. Mosley 8-13-1859 (9-4-1859)
Majors, Harriet to Charles Barton 12-27-1870 (12-31-1870) B
Majors, Louisa to W. N. Johnson 6-11-1870 (6-16-1870)
Majors, Mary A. E. to G. B. Nicholson 9-21-1859 (9-23-1859)
Majors, Racheal to Henry Elliott 12-25-1873 (12-26-1873) B
Majors, Rebecca to John T. Hooper 11-14-1859 (11-16-1859)
Mallery, Anna R. to J. W. Chambliss 12-20-1876 (12-21-1876)
Mallery, Mary to George Wells 9-12-1866 (9-20-1866) B
Mallory, Alta to H. C. Flintoff 12-26-1874 (12-28-1874)
Mallory, Harriet to Richard Watson 2-28-1873 (3-1-1873) B
Mallory, Mahala to Andrew Dowlen 7-28-1879 B
Mallory, Roena P. to W. L. Garrett 2-9-1857 (2-15-1857)
Malory, Sarah V. to J. P. Vaughan 6-15-1861 (6-18-1861)
Manwarin, Henrietta to J. J. Gray 11-8-1879 (11-9-1879)
Martin, Adaline to Albin G. Drake 7-14-1856
Martin, Cornela to Isaac W. Sanders 2-2-1872 (2-4-1872)
Martin, Nancy to A. M. Gower 10-5-1859
Mathas, June to L. Galligan 10-25-1876
Maxey, M. A. H. to Wm. H. Wall 1-6-1876
Maxey, Mary W. to W. H. Walker 12-4-1879
Maxey, Susannah to J. D. Smith 12-4-1871 (12-8-1871)
Mays, Caroline to John M. Bagwell 9-7-1859 (9-8-1859)
Mays, Frances C. to C. H. Haskins 9-17-1862 (10-26-1862)
Mays, Martha to John S. Halley 3-28-1857 (3-29-1857)
Mays, Susan to A. W. Crocker 11-14-1861
Mays, Telitha to John H. Clark 3-1-1871
McCall, Sallie to Masha C. Read 11-16-1870 (11-17-1870)
McCarrall, Margret J. to Stephen A. M. Elliott 3-11-1870
McCarrol, Eliz. A. to John M. Elliott 9-4-1867 (8-5-1867)
McCay, Lucinda to Henry Adams 9-1-1864
McClure, Musedore to Wm. H. Owen 7-25-1866
McCormac, Mattie to Alva Hollis 2-17-1881 (2-20-1881)
McCormack, E. to G. Godsey 7-20-857
McCormack, E. C. to Elisha Smith 11-12-1860 (11-15-1860)
McCormack, Josephine to A. W. Sanders 10-21-1875 (10-22-1875)
McCormack, L. A. to Leonidas Hunt 4-4-1857
McCormack, Louisa to C. A. Harper 5-10-1864
McCormack, Malvina to David A. Boyt 12-7-1876 (12-8-1876)
McCormack, Mary J. to H.U. Adkins 2-5-1867 (2-6-1867)
McCormack, Narcissa to Jessee Harrel no date (with Jan 1873)
McCormick, Sallie to B. B. Binkley 7-27-1864 (7-28-1864)
McCorrall, N. E. to T. M. Trulove 7-25-1865 (7-26-1865)
McDaniel, Annie M. to Z. W. Owen 10-24-1879 (10-26-1879)
McDaniel, M. W. to C. R. Farmer 3-29-1879 (3-30-1879)
McDaniel, Nancy J. to J. T. Woodson 6-26-1875
McDaniel, Permelia to Stephen B. Hale 3-20-1857 (3-22-1857)
McDaniel, Rebecca to Montgomery Nicholson 1-5-1871
McFall, Susan to S. W. Newton 10-29-1874
McGowen, Ellen to Peter Wilson 8-1-1879 B
McLaughlin, Ophelia to A. W. Stuart 5-24-1879 (5-27-1879)
McNeal, America to Wm. Murry McNeal 10-20-1874
McTulere?, Samuella to Wm. H. Pack 2-11-1873 (2-13-1873)
Mecaba, Elizabeth to John A. Hagewood 12-31-1856 (12-30?-1856)

Mickle, Fredonia to G. W. Hiland 12-14-1874 (12-15-1874)
Miles, Adaline T. to Albert Smith 4-2-1862 (4-3-1862)
Miles, C. H. to E. W. Fetts 11-21-1857
Miles, Elizabeth to Geo. W. Basford 11-15-1858 (11-17-1858)
Miles, Elizabeth O. to Thomas A. Doke 11-3-1873 (11-9-1873)
Miles, Fredonia to R. J. Watts 11-12-1879 (11-6?-1879)
Miles, H. C. to A. G. Crantz 9-18-1870
Miles, Louisa to B. J. Stack 12-23-1859
Miles, Martha A. to John G. Curtis 10-25-1858 (10-27-1858)
Miles, Martha A. to James S.? Simmons 1-12-1881 (1-13-1881)
Miles, Mary to James W. Smith 11-4-1862
Miles, Mary to M. W. Webb 9-4-1876
Miles, N. N. to B. C. Morris 2-6-1861 (2-8-1861)
Miles, Nancy to Wm. J. Bobbett 1-2-1867 (1-3-1867)
Miles, Nannie to James Eatherly 3-6-1878
Miles, Sarah C. to J. M. Osborn 1-28-1874
Miles, Tennessee to Frank Pool 12-28-1859 (12-26?-1859)
Miller, Delila to William Reman 2-24-1874 (2-26-1874)
Millikin, Lucy to W. S. Roop? 7-9-1879 (7-10-1879)
Minor, Lizzie to Wm. Hooper 11-13-1879 (11-15-1879) B
Mitchel, Francis to W. M. Walker 12-20-1878 (12-24-1878)
Mitchel, Lucy to Fate Perry 12-20-1878 (12-21-1878)
Monroe, Ida to Jesse B. Hagewood 12-24-1874
Moore, Cyntha to Littleton Perry 8-11-1857
Moore, Josephine to J. J. Evans 4-26-1869 (4-29-1869)
Moore, Julia A. to M. Perry 10-18-1866 (10-19-1866)
Moore, Louisa to Benja. Paschal 1-4-1860 (1-6-1860)
Moore, Martha J. to Jasper Ridge 3-23-1864
Moore, Mollie J. to Wm. Riggan 2-8-1881 (2-10-1881)
Moore, T. J. to F. G. Carney 10-2-1858
More, Mary to Joseph Gattis 9-5-1867
Morgan, Martha E. to Elijah A. Stewart 11-13-1866
Morris, Charlotte F. to A. M. Binkley 10-2-1869 (10-3-1869)
Morris, Eliza to John R. Binkley 5-19-1866 (5-20-1866)
Morris, Elizabeth to H. W. Binkley 9-23-1867 (9-2?-1867)
Morris, F. P. to S. W. Fizer 1-6-1872 (1-7-1872)
Morris, Frances to R. B. Knight 10-6-1870
Morris, L. E. to D. A. Hunter 12-19-1859
Morris, M. E. to C. W. Sterry 12-12-1877 (12-13-1877)
Morris, M. F. to E. D. Leeter 4-16-1857
Morris, M. J. to Joseph Grant 11-19-1859 (11-26-1859)
Morris, Marinda to Alexa Redman 10-20-1877 (10-21-1877) B
Morris, Mary to Henry Binkley 2-5-1876 (2-6-1876)
Morris, Mary to T. J. Puckett 12-20-1864
Morris, Melvina A. to Joshuwa Morris 4-12-1862
Morris, Sarah to Walton Crunk 12-5-1868 (12-6-1868)
Morris, Sarah to Benjamin Demumbra 10-14-1876 (10-15-1876)
Morris, Susan J. to J. R. Allen 9-14-1880 (9-16-1880)
Morris, Tabitha to Jacob Bennett 1-17-1857 (1-18-1857)
Morriss, Elmina to Jessie L. Owen 10-15-1874
Morton, F. to James Alley 1-11-1857 (1-15-1857)
Mosier, Elizabeth to Jacob Bennett 7-8-1865
Mosier, W. A. to Jessee Bennett 2-10-1866
Muellins, Betsy Jane to Daniel R. Hutton 5-19-1874 (5-20-1874)

Murff, Elizabeth A. to William F. McGhee 7-27-1869 (7-28-1869)
Murff, R. T. to T. J. Shaw 12-2-1871 (12-3-1871)
Murphey, E. J. to T. W. Hunter 10-27-1857 (10-29-1857)
Murphey, Mary A. to Scott Nicholson 5-12-1871
Murphy, F. to M. V. B. Walker 2-10-1858
Naney, M. R. to H. R. Pool 6-17-1858
Naney, Mary a. to Eliza Hall 7-19-1862 (7-23-1862)
Nanney, Emma to C. J. Hollis 1-19-1880
Nanney, O. to Wm. Edger 3-24-1880 (3-25-1880)
Nannie, Josephine to D. L. Price 3-6-1868 (3-8-1868)
Neal, Alice M. to Allen T. Thompson 2-13-1872 (2-15-1872)
Neal, Jane S. to John Walker 11-25-1865 B
Neal, Mary E. to W. S. Smith 12-6-1866
Neal, Susan A. to Wm. W. Thompson 12-6-1866
Neighbors, Martha A. to Marion Curtis 5-30-1870 (6-11-1870)
Neighbors, Mary to Alexander Bean 11-1-1875 (11-3-1875)
Nelson, M. A. to Avis Brown 2-18-1867 (2-21-1867)
Nelson, Sarah to Joseph Brown 11-18-1871 (11-26-1871)
Newland, Mary E. to W. H. Buckley 11-30-1878 (12-1-1878)
Newlin, Nannie E. to W. J. Shearon 10-27-1877 (10-28-1877)
Newman, Ellen to R. K. Brown 11-5-1879
Newman, Judah A. to Mike Krantz 1-28-1871
Newman, Martha to T. M. Binkley 8-5-1876 (8-7-1876)
Newman, Mary to Isaac Darrow 5-15-1872 (5-16-1872)
Newman, Susan T. to James Young 2-17-1865
Newsom, C. H. to G. P. Mallory 2-7-1876 (2-10-1876)
Newsom, Elizabeth to F. B. Howe 12-18-1866 (12-19-1866)
Newsom, Emaline to George Kellum 4-19-1867 (4-20-1867) B
Newsom, Martha to Thomas F. Hutton 3-18-1865
Newsom, Sallie E. to W. D. Cherry 10-18-1867
Newsom, Sarah to Ephraim Woodward 1-2-1874 (1-3-1874) B
Nichol, Fanny to W. C. Hooper 8-15-1871
Nichol, Viola to G. D. Hudsan 2-15-1879 (no return)
Nichols, Berty to Peter Balthrop 11-27-1874 (11-28-1874) B
Nichols, Cornelius T. to W. T. Gower 10-16-1876 (10-19-1876)
Nichols, Cresia to E. F. Harris 2-8-1866
Nichols, Ellen to Mathew T. Harris 8-21-1867 (8-22-1867)
Nichols, Fannie to James Lauson 3-31-1871 B
Nichols, Ferebee to Felix Ellis 4-9-1872 (4-10-1872) B
Nichols, Georg A. to Joseph Harris 9-6-1870 (9-7-1870)
Nichols, Mehaly C. to John T. Fambrough 7-22-1868 (7-23-1868)
Nichols, Nancy E. to W. J. Shivers 6-3-1872 (6-16-1872)
Nichols, Rebecca J. to D. H. Demumbra 12-23-1872 (11-13-1872)
Nicholsen, Mary to Robert McCormack 10-12-1876
Nicholson, A. T. to D. B. Nicholson 10-24-1876 (10-25-1876)
Nicholson, Adaline to William Henderson 7-6-1868 (7-11-1868) B
Nicholson, Cyntha A. to T. R. Owens 1-28-1868
Nicholson, D. A. to John F. Mosley 2-14-1860 (2-16-1860)
Nicholson, E. B. to W. T. Bailey 12-27-1873 (12-28-1873)
Nicholson, Eliza to Rufus Jackson 4-27-1867 (4-28-1867)
Nicholson, Fredonia to Eli Harris 7-31-1857 (8-3-1857)
Nicholson, J. G. to J. R. Rudolph 12-16-1857 (12-17-1857)
Nicholson, Mary to Doss Humphreys 1-1-1875 B
Nicholson, Mary T. to W. Whitworth 8-7-1880 (8-15-1880)

Nicholson, P. G. to T. B. Perdue 11-29-1866
Nicholson, Rowena L. to B. H. Maran 11-25-1879 (11-26-1879)
Nicholson, Susan A. to Isaac A. Coon 12-25-1870 (1-1-1871)
Nickens, R. S. to William Humbold 3-13-1857 (3-17-1857)
Nickolson, Chyntha? to T. R. Owens 1-27-1868
Nickolson, E. N. to G. B. Nickolson 1-8-1868 (1-9-1868)
Nickolson, Korrener? C. to W. H. Crotzer 2-10-1868 (2-11-1868)
Nicks, Tennessee to George M. Stovall 1-7-1869
Noe, AlliceM. to Joh Farner 4-8-1871 (4-9-1871)
Nye, M. A. to J. M. Kirkpatrick 2-12-1880
O'Brien, Mary to W. W. Sanders 3-8-1875 (3-9-1875)
Oakley, Mandy to Charles Frazier 7-29-1880 (7-30-1880) B
Obrien, Nannie to G. W. Boyte 3-16-1878
Oliver, Matilda to Joseph Krantz 9-21-1875 (9-23-1875)
Olliver, D. P. to George W. Perry 7-13-1872 (7-14-1872)
Osborne, Eury F. to George P. Finch 11-5-1877 (11-13-1877)
Osborne, M. A. to Z. T. Hutton 4-23-1865
Overton, Perlina to Lewis Allen 9-16-1869 B
Owen, Sarah A. to Andrew Hamilton 12-12-1876
Ozburn, Martha J. to John J. Smith 2-3-1879 (2-13-1879)
Ozburn, Serena E. to Samuel J. Brinkley 1-13-1876
Pace, Martha A. to John Evilcizer 6-30-1869 (7-3-1869)
Pace, Mary T. to John T. Jackson 12-28-1867
Pace, Nancy to S. A. Nicholson 11-18-1875
Pace, Sarah H. to William H. Hall 10-6-1870 (10-7-1870)
Pack, M. M. to J. B. Bell 1-17-1876 (1-19-1876)
Page, H. A. to J. Morris 1-24-1880 (1-25-1880)
Page, Julia to Henry Dozier 10-19-1869 (10-20-1869) B
Pardue, Emer to Benjamin Hunter 10-25-1872 (10-26-1872) B
Pardue, Katie to Elick Smith 12-25-1873 (12-27-1873) B
Pardue, Mary E. to Thos. A. Turner 11-22-1870 (11-23-1870)
Pardue, Mattie A. to James E. Cozo? 11-16-1868 (11-17-1868)
Parrish, Jane to Wm. H. Oliver 7-13-1869
Parry, Sarah P. to J.J. Stewart 11-16-1859 (11-17-1859)
Pascal, Louisa to James Basford 7-5-1877 (7-31-1877)
Paterson, Sarah to George Pack 11-1-1872 (10?-3-1872) B
Patterson, E. to F. Miner? 12-26-1876 B
Patterson, Telulia J. to B. H. Hagewood 12-19-1877 (12-20-1877)
Patterson, Virginia to Thomas Washington 6-13-1876 B
Pattin, Judith to James H. Boyle 7-15-1880
Patton, Sarah A. to G. W. Simmons 11-8-1865
Peebles, Harriett C. to James J. Lenox 1-10-1860
Pegram, Bettie to Aris Brown 8-29-1863 (8-3?-1863)
Pegram, Billie F. to James Walkup 12-3-1860 (12-20-1860)
Pegram, Creecy to Andrew Huddleston 10-16-1867 (10-19-1867) B
Pegram, Judith A. to William Holt 1-30-1864 (2-4-1864)
Pegram, Julia A. to W. C. Hutton 7-1-1862
Pegram, Penina to Joseph Mays 8-24-1870 (8-28-1870)
Pegram, Sarah F. to C. F. Brown 10-18-1862
Pennington, Craleney A. to Levi Hyde 8-6-1872 (8-7-1872) B
Pennington, Elizabeth to Jacob Whitehead 1-24-1870 (1-30-1870)
Pennington, Mary to W. R. Fort 7-4-1872
Pentecast, E. M. to W. H. Pentecast 1-4-1859
Perdue, Aquilla to W. H. Miles 1-23-1867 (1-24-1867)

Perdue, Elizabeth H. to A. T. Shores 2-25-1861
Perdue, M. C. to D. J. Justice 8-3-1858
Perdue, Nancy to Dick Follis 1-13-1875 (1-14-1875) B
Perdue, Nannie to Jordan Smith 12-29-1866 B
Perdue, Sarah M. to Greene W. Hunt 1-18-1870
Perkins, Martha Jane to William McRussell 4-5-1871 (4-6-1871)
Perkins, Mary to Isaac Van Vaulkinburgh 9-1-1873
Perry, Lydia A. to Patrick Galligan 5-14-1866 (5-13?-1866)
Perry, M. J. to ---san Eastridge 11-1-1878 (11-10-1878)
Perry, Martha to A. J. Sanders 1-27-1858
Perry, Martha to James Simmons 11-20-1875 (11-21-1875)
Perry, Mary Ann to Henry Holt 2-13-1875 (2-14-1875)
Perry, Mollie to George Harrington 5-30-1872 (6-2-1872)
Pinson, M. J. to B. F. Fielder 4-28-1869 (4-29-1869)
Pinson, Nancy to Thomas W. Gupton 9-13-1866 (9-16-1866)
Pool, George Ann T. to John A. Pool 11-11-1868 (11-12-1868)
Pool, Rosa to A. R. Cam 10-14-1869
Pool, Sally to B. F. Harris 9-21-1880
Pool, Sarah M. to James W. Bright 11-29-1873 (11-30-1873)
Pool, Verginia T. to John J. Cain 12-25-1871 (12-26-1871)
Pool, Victoria to A.N. Cain 8-18-1859 (8-1?-1859)
Pool, Y.? W. to John Batts 12-23-1857
Porch, Deborah E. to William J. Pegram 2-4-1865 (2-5-1868)
Porch, M. C. to L. G. Meriham 2-5-1868 (2-7-1868)
Porter, Mary M. to Samuel H. Corsan 2-5-1868 (3-5-1868)
Power, Bettie to Wesley Head 7-17-1879 B
Prescott, Mariah L. to Isaac N. Jones 7-4-1859
Pulley, M. J. to W. H. Brown 4-11-1874 (5-16-1874)
Purnell, Martha to William Price 2-16-1864
Rack, Frances to William Russell 5-12-1860
Ralls, Luella L. to Charles Dowlen 3-24-1871 (3-28-1871)
Ramer, Dicy E. to Eli M. Ramer 12-2-1869
Ramer, Nancy to William W. Bone 10-15-1864
Ramer, Sally G. to John F. Knight 4-8-1870 (4-10-1870)
Ramer, Sarah to James Knight 1-9-1860 (1-13-1860)
Randle, Melissa to Henry W. Puckett 7-4-1878 (no return)
Randolph, M. J. to W. L. Neblett 1-14-1857 (1-20-1857)
Ranor, Elizabeth to John F. Nighs? 11-22-1878
Ray, Fannie to Doc Harper 4-8-1881 (4-10-1881)
Raymer, Mary F. to Joseph Hampton 12-15-1877 (no return)
Raymer, Milberry to John M. Raymer 1-26-1878 (1-27-1878)
Read, Elizabeth to Walter G. Gray 8-11-1880 (8-12-1880)
Read, L. A. to M. M. Chambliss 11-19-1872 (11-20-1872)
Read, Metilda to William Carter 12-22-1866 (12-25-1866) B
Read, N. A. R. F. to N. N. Binkley 12-12-1857
Read, Nancy E. to James Binkley 9-3-1859 (9-4-1859)
Read, Sarah to Timothy Eastridge 7-13-1871 (7-16-1871)
Reece, Elizabeth L. to P. C. Shearron 1-1-1868
Reed, Harret to John M. Brown 9-11-1873
Reggan, Annie T. to James Dillingham 1-20-1878
Richardson, Sarah A. to Preston Krantz 10-27-1870 (10-30-1870)
Richardson, Sarah E. to James M. Perdue 5-31-1877 (6-31?-1877)
Riggan, Alice G. to Wm. T. Dunn 9-23-1876 (9-26-1876)
Riggan, Annie A. to J. C. Medows 12-10-1874 (12-15-1874)

Riggan, Emma D. to T. S. Hooper 12-29-1879 (12-31-1879)
Riggan, F. A. to Joseph Dozier 1-23-1879 (1-26-1879)
Riggan, Harriett A. to Rufus Turner 1-5-1870 (1-6-1870)
Riggan, Mary E. to H. C. Dozier 8-12-1876
Riggin, M. J. to J. B. Hooper 9-15-1865 (9-27-1865)
Riggin, Mary A. to C. S. Hooper 9-25-1865 (9-27-1865)
Robertson, Harret to Berry Huddleston 11-13-1873 (11-14-1873) B
Robertson, Jenney to Phillip Collier 12-24-1873 (12-26-1873) B
Robertson, Margaret to Frank Newsom 1-25-1873 B
Robertson, Mary to Robert Gorden 6-1-1872 (6-2-1872) B
Robertson, Mary to R. W. Williams 10-6-1869
Robertson, Sefrona to Samuel Washington 10-13-1877 B
Robinson, Hettie to James Hardeman 9-11-1876 B
Rogers, Anna J. to J. O. R. Hooper 9-18-1866
Roope, Geneva to John H. Hameris? 3-23-1867
Rose, Eliz. to John Bess 12-2-1857
Rose, M. A. to G. W. Binkley 7-20-1859 (7-21-1859)
Rose, Nannie to Thomas Krantz 12-23-1876
Rose, Sarah F. to Thomas Carney 2-3-1872 (2-4-1872)
Ross, Catharine to F. M. Copley 12-25-1867
Ross, Eveline V. to John J. Dortch 5-23-1868 (5-24-1868)
Rosson, Jennie A. to Henry T. Williams 4-29-1870
Rudelph, Loucretia to J. J. Wilson 1-6-1874 (1-8-1874)
Rukes, Arrilla to G. W. Burton 10-12-1857 (10-13-1857)
Russell, Cornelia to G. jr. Greene 9-16-1872
Russell, Katie to J. A. Higgins 2-15-1875
Russell, L. to Wm. Jackson 7-6-1857 (7-9-1857)
Russell, Maggie to John Appleton 6-23-1875
Russell, Missouri J. to William Brown 1-6-1863
Russell, Sarah W. to D. C. Stewart 12-18-1876 (12-24-1876)
Ryman, Delilah to J. P. Vick 12-30-1879
Sample, Emeline to J. T. Pentecost 10-31-1868 (11-17-1868)
Sander, Emily R. to J. J. Everett 1-27-1869 (1-28-1869)
Sanderlin, Bettie to T. D. Hunter 12-20-1873 (12-23-1873)
Sanders, A. T. to W. J. Boyte 6-29-1872 (6-30-1872)
Sanders, Elmina to David A. Wall 1-13-1874
Sanders, Jennie L. to J. D. Arrington 8-25-1869
Sanders, Lucy A. to Wm. Eatherly 2-19-1867 (2-21-1867)
Sanders, Luvenia to Z. T. Harris 1-8-1874 (1-11-1874)
Sanders, M. to Jas. W. Pool 8-13-1857
Sanders, Martha J. to W. H. Harris 8-21-1869 (8-22-1869)
Sanders, Mary E. to T. P. Bradley 2-17-1869 (2-18-1869)
Sanders, Mary N. to Isaac Wilson 12-23-1869
Sanders, Nancy D. to Jasper Simmons 3-1-1863 (3-3-1863)
Sanders, Sarah F. to G. W. Read 12-24-1870 (12-28-1870)
Sanders, Susan to Martin Shadrick 7-12-1871
Sanders, Susan R. to H. J. Binkley 8-3-1872 (8-4-1872)
Sawyer, Patsey to Alexander Harris 4-4-1880 B
Scott, Annie to B. F. Hannah 1-19-1867
Scott, Annie to Benjamin F. Hannah 4-4-1868 (4-5-1868)
Scott, Fannie F. to W. W. Deal 5-11-1861
Scott, Fannie F. to W. W. Deal 5-11-1861
Seals, Martha S. to L. D. Buckhannan 12-9-1874 (12-13-1874)
Setton, Elizabeth T. to G. W. Craig 6-22-1878 (no return)

Sewell, Milley to George Harris 12-23-1874
Shafara?, Martha J. to Lee Watson 12-2-1880
Shaw, Ann to Claiborne Shearin 11-24-1866 (11-26-1866) B
Shaw, Eliza to Jack Powel 12-26-1878 B
Shaw, Eliza to Joran Smith 5-24-1872 B
Shaw, Mary to Richard Hunt 1-13-1870 B
Shaw, N. E. to R. S. Freeman 10-16-1878 (10-17-1878)
Shearen, Bettie to J. T. Shaw 12-23-1876 (12-24-1876)
Shearin, Mahala to Thomas Fordner 3-11-1876 B
Shearon, Addie to James Smith 12-23-1880
Shearon, Ann E. to T. Hu Hudgens 1-14-1867
Shearon, Eller to J. B. Davis 9-1-1877 (9-2-1877)
Shearon, Emily R. to Geo. W. Harris 7-9-1861
Shearon, H. R. to J. H. Wall 2-8-1881 (2-9-1881)
Shearon, Isabel to Charley Clark 2-2-1874 (3-7-1875?) B
Shearon, Margret to Luke Patterson 6-14-1879 B
Shearon, Martha to J. B. Nicholson 11-26-1879 (11-30-1879)
Shearon, Mary to R. T. Harris 6-5-1880 (6-6-1880)
Shearon, N. W. to Henry J. Shaw 4-11-1859 (4-12-1859)
Shearon, Shosie to Perry Williams 5-?-1880 B
Shearron, Martha to Benjamin W. Hudgens 12-3-1868 (12-4-1868)
Sheeran, Harriet to Booker Stewart 12-28-1876 B
Shelton, Caity to Walker Smith 4-18-1874 (4-19-1874) B
Shelton, Clarice? to Newton Newsom 4-24-1880 (4-25-1880) B
Shelton, Lucy to Solomon Newsom 2-2-1874 (2-14-1874) B
Shelton, Martha to Taylor Dunkin 12-30-1871 B
Shelton, Rosanah to Oliver Henry 3-3-1871 B
Shelton, Rose to Anthony Armstead 12-15-1877 (12-16-1877) B
Shelton, Susan to Simon Hollensworth 12-7-1878 (12-8-1878) B
Sheron, F. to L. C. Grey 4-28-1877 (4-29-1877)
Sherron, Hester to Ben Hudgens 2-19-1870 (3-6-1870) B
Sherron, Nancy to Thomas Boyd 4-7-1873 (4-9-1873)
Sherron, Rosanna to J. C. York 11-23-1872 (11-24-1872)
Sherron, Spatia to Frank Parkerson 12-18-1874 B
Shrockley, L. to S. C. Brown 11-1-1862
Shubert, Alice E. to James Ivey 4-27-1871 (4-30-1871)
Shubert, M. E. to O. D. Jackson 10-30-1858
Shumake, Harriet to Thomas Dickerson 6-24-1870 (6-26-1870)
Simmons, Eller to E. B. jr. Carney 6-9-1873 (6-15-1873)
Simmons, Margret to J. P. B. Henderson 7-4-1859 (7-6-1859)
Simmons, Martha J. to John W. Sanders 2-21-1874 (2-22-1874)
Simmons, Mary E. to James A. Dozier 1-8-1874
Simmons, N. E. to W. R. Dowlen 12-9-1878 (12-11-1878)
Simmons, Nancy J. to L. S.? Bobbitt 1-27-1876 (1-30-1876)
Simpkins, E. to C. Cagle 12-23-1876 (12-24-1876)
Simpkins, Martha J. to J. G. Simpkins 4-12-1877
Simpkins, Sarah A. to W. C. Head 11-15-1875 (11-18-1875)
Simpkins, Sarah A. to F. M. Proctor 3-12-1866
Simpson, H. to E. E. Thompson 1-12-1859 (1-13-1859)
Simpson, Mary L. to Ralph Shevers 4-30-1872 (5-5-1872)
Simpson, Nancy to G. W. Darrow 9-21-1875
Sisler?, M. T. to W. M. Askins 2-10-1872 (2-11-1872)
Sittner?, Nancy to John Nunley 5-25-1868 (5-26-1868)
Sloan, M. C. to R. B. Sloan 9-18-1857

Slump, Celestea P. to Henry H. Ragan 10-14-1873 (10-13?-1873)
Slump, Maggie Jane to B. P. Lovell 11-17-1879 (11-19-1879)
Slump, Martha E. to W. H. Hicks 8-4-1880
Smith, Allice to Charley M. Turner 3-8-1871
Smith, Ann to B. M. Davis 11-17-1865
Smith, Bettie to C. H. Patrick 6-8-1881 (6-10-1881)
Smith, C. C. to J. L. Pack 3-17-1863
Smith, Charlotte to Thos. C. Barclift 1-4-1858 (1-5-1858)
Smith, E. P. to James T. Mays 12-6-1860 (12-11-1860)
Smith, Elizabeth to Y. W. Benningfield 2-21-1868 (2-25-1868)
Smith, Elizabeth to Thos. Sisler 10-21-1880 (10-24-1880)
Smith, L. C. to T. J. Hagewood 6-10-1873
Smith, Levina E. to Henry Stalzey 11-14-1859
Smith, M. E. to L. L. Pack 3-5-1877 (3-7-1877)
Smith, M. M. to Q. E. Heflin 1-29-1874
Smith, Martha V. to George F. Binkley 11-17-1873 (12-19-1873)
Smith, Mary E. to W. C. Perdue 12-28-1859
Smith, Rebecca to J. W. Sanders 7-7-1876 (7-16-1876)
Smith, Roxzaner to Levingston Binkley 6-12-1869
Smith, S. E. to G. P. Woodward 6-8-1861 (6-9-1861)
Smith, Sarah A. to O. Edwards 8-18-1863
Smith, Susan to James Sheppard 3-14-1872 B
Smith, Viola L. to C. J. Hagewood 12-20-1873 (12-30-1873)
Sneed, Selina J. to Charles B. Lovell 12-16-1867 (12-19-1867)
Spates, Charity to Guss Shaw 6-8-1872 (6-9-1872) B
Speight, Bedy to Price Huett 12-23-1875 (12-22?-1875) B
Speight, Emma to Solomon Wall 8-18-1877 B
Stack, Ivory? G. to James H. Reed 8-26-1874 (8-31-1874)
Stack, Katie to D. J. Elliott 12-8-1877 (12-13-1877)
Stack, M. M. to Ed A. Wheeler 5-28-1858 (6-4-1858)
Stack, Mary to J.F. Watts 3-20-1876 (3-29-1876)
Stack, Mary E. to E. R. Calor 9-3-1874
Stack, Sarah A to R. M. Bethune 1-1-1868 (1-2-1868)
Stack, Virginia to H. W. Baggett 10-26-1878 (10-31-1878)
Stewart, Addie J. to S. B. Smith 5-20-1874
Stewart, Ellen to Frank Jones 1-1-1874 (1-2-1874) B
Stewart, Evaline to W. H. H. Gent 11-10-1858 (11-11-1858)
Stewart, Freedonia to F. H. Cabler 5-1-1858 (5-6-1858)
Stewart, G. A. to B. J. Barnes 1-3-1859 (1-4-1859)
Stewart, Izora? to Adam Binkley 11-14-1866 (11-15-1866)
Stewart, Jane to Thomas B. Perdue 12-28-1868 (12-29-1868)
Stewart, L. L. to H. D. Caragen 12-18-1880 (12-19-1880)
Stewart, Margret to J. W. Stewart 9-28-1869 (10-30-1869)
Stewart, Martha to E. W. Carney 11-25-1869
Stewart, Mary to M. Haris 12-16-1867 (12-18-1867)
Stewart, Mary J. to J. R. Stuart 10-2-1871 (10-4-1871)
Stewart, Nancy M. to J. P. Moran 2-5-1858
Stewart, P. A. to J. R. P. Carney 12-28-1865 (2-6-1867?)
Stewart, Permelia to H. W. Miles 4-12-1869 (4-13-1869)
Stewart, Rebecca to B. B. Bright 7-15-1857 (8-3-1857)
Stewart, Sallie to Edward Ned Head 3-22-1873 B
Stewart, Sarah to Newsom Harris 4-24-1858 (4-25-1858)
Stewart, Sarah E. to J. D. Bobbitt 11-25-1870 (11-27-1870)
Stinnett, Nannie E. to W. J. Dillingham 10-25-1875 (10-27-1875)

Stinnett, Sarah A. to Peter Andrews 3-6-1877 (3-7-1877)
Stokes, Frances to Richard Brown 8-27-1878 B
Story, Annie H. to C. C. Hall 11-5-1878
Story, Toonothy? to W. C. Dozier 10-21-1875
Stovall, Nancy E. to D. B. S. Tally 12-3-1859
Stringfellow, Elvira to Alfred Howel 8-27-1863
Stringfellow, Lucy to William Harper 12-21-1871 (12-29-1871)
Stringfellow, Margret L. to R. J. Stringfellow 10-24-1869
Stuart, Mattie to R. M. Swan 2-19-1868 (2-20-1868)
Stump, Christianna to Samuel D. Watkins 2-27-1873 (3-2-1873)
Stump?, Julia to S. J. Watkins 10-17-1866
Sullivan, Kate to Henry Simmons 7-27-1870 (8-31-1870)
Sutton, Mary E. to Edward B. McFarlin 5-5-1858 (5-6-1858)
Swaggart, E. J. to Wm. Simmons 4-11-1859 (4-14-1859)
Swan, Malinda to Joseph M. Phillips 6-5-1875
Swar, Emily to sGeo. W. Rasberry 4-18-1859 (4-19-1859)
Sweat, Martha to Elijah Mathews 8-13-1878 B
Sweney, Mary Ann to R. M. Pack 6-2-1863
Swift, Samantha to R. B. Baggett 10-13-1879 (10-15-1879)
Symes, Emaline A. to Charles M. Stuart 10-15-1859 (10-16-1859)
Talley, M. E. to Jas. C. Crenshaw 1-11-1861
Talley, Mortica E. to James C. Crenshaw 1-11-1861
Tally, Emer to Granvill Cuningham 2-2-1872 (2-4-1872) B
Tate, Eliza to Isaac E. Paradise 3-13-1877
Teasley, Almedia to J. W. Wilson 3-2-1872 (3-3-1872)
Teasley, Amy to Moses Williams 1-21-1873 B
Teasley, Anacha? to Jesse Nicholson 5-21-1873 B
Teasley, Ella? to Samuel Hunter 9-10-1870 B
Teasley, G. F. to W. H. Plasters 1-11-1860 (1-12-1860)
Teasley, Jeridine to W. H. Pool 11-30-1872 (12-1-1872)
Teasley, Louvendy F. to Jas. B. Maxey 12-21-1878 (12-22-1878)
Teasley, Lucy H. to William Sterry? 11-18-1871 (11-19-1871)
Teasley, M. A. to T. J. Pace 1-6-1879 (1-8-1879)
Teasley, Mary to John K. Hunt 11-26-1872
Teasley, Mary to J. C. Shearon 11-22-1877
Teasley, N. J. to T. R. Harris 1-7-1876 (1-9-1876)
Teasley, Nancy to T. E. Walker 1-3-1876
Teasley, Nancy J. to Wm. D. Weakley 1-12-1859 (1-13-1859)
Teasley, P. T. to G. W. Wall 3-29-1876 (3-30-1876)
Teasley, Sallie A. to Benjamin Teasley 1-30-1871 (2-2-1871) B
Teasly, Lucinda to M. H. Sanders 8-15-1877 (8-16-1877)
Teasly, Mary A. to James T. Shaw 12-17-1867 (12-19-1867)
Temple, Lucy to Wyatt Lee 3-20-1869 (3-24-1869) B
Templeton, Mary to James Campbell 4-21-1864
Tettar?, Martha Jane to John H. Boling 7-6-1872 (7-7-1872)
Thaxton, Jemima to John Hollis 4-15-1859 (4-17-1859)
Thaxton, Mary J. to James H. Cain 3-3-1858 (3-4-1858)
Thenabee?, Eliz. to Mathew Satterfield 2-24-1857 (5-31-1857)
Thomas, Manerva to Jordan Canady 12-21-1874 B
Thompson, Malinda to Martin Holt 10-13-1873 B
Thompson, Mary E. to Benjamin C. Hawkins 2-20-1861
Thompson, Nancy to Wade M. Johns 3-17-1864 (3-18-1864)
Thompson, Parile to Alford Williams 5-1-1875 B
Thompson, Priscilla to George M. Elliott 9-3-1858 (9-4-1858)

Tomlin, Bettie to M. S. Wyatt 5-5-1874
Trainum, Eller to J. J. Basford 10-4-1869 (10-14-1869)
Turner, Martha E. to Gustavus Dunn 11-6-1872
Turner, Mary to Absalum Page 12-29-1859
Turner, Susan to James H. Anderson 12-24-1859
Turner, Susan A. to W. T. Clark 11-6-1863
Turntine, E. J. to Smith Rooper 7-16-1867 (SB 1857?)
Tymms, Rebecca E. to John G. Greene 8-18-1860 (8-19-1860)
Ussery, Amanda to Thomas Woodward 9-18-1876 (9-26-1876) B
Ussery, Bettie to Green Greer 11-29-1876 (11-30-1876) B
Ussery, E. J. to James H. Fulghum 7-29-1857 (10-4-1857)
Ussery, Mary A. to James H. Fulghum 5-22-1865
Ussery, Mary E. to J.M. Hooper 12-22-1866 (12-26-1866)
Ussery, Nancy F. to G. G. Wyndham 12-19-1866
Ussery, Susan to Thomas Mays 1-9-1873 B
Ussery, Susan to Isham Pack 1-3-1876 B
Ussey, Susan to Thomas Mays 1-11-1873 B
Vanhook, C. J. to G. W. Shearon 11-18-1880
Vanhook, Caroline to Peter Wilson 10-6-1866 B
Vanhook, Sarah E. to R. M. Knox 4-20-1876 (4-26-1876)
Vanvolkenberg, Sarah M. to T. Elliott 2-26-1862 (3-2-1862)
Ventress, Susan E. to J. J. Bennett 11-26-1879
Vess, Mary to Lewis Perry 6-24-1874 (6-26-1874)
Vick, Dilcy E. to William M. Hooper 11-26-1866
Vick, Elizabeth to Isaac W. Nabors 10-25-1858
Vick, Martha to T. W. Russell 7-27-1863
Vick, Mary J. to Daniel Brown 10-1-1857
Vick, Susana to W. A. Biggs 1-15-1872 (1-14?-1872)
Walden, Texas to Lewis Perry 10-1-1873
Walker, A. to Jesse Hyde 8-23-1867 (8-25-1867) B
Walker, Amanda E. to W. T. Bell 2-13-1873
Walker, Barber A. to Alick Balden 4-23-1870 (5-1-1870)
Walker, E. G. to W. S. Shearon 12-15-1877 (12-20-18877)
Walker, E. T. to J. A. Justice 3-17-1868
Walker, Elizabeth K. to H. C. Fox 1-28-1873 (1-29-1873)
Walker, Elvira to C. W. Starns 7-18-1857 (7-19-1857)
Walker, Emily L. to H. P. Krantz 12-4-1879
Walker, G. A. E. to Jas. W. Johnson 3-4-1858 (3-7-1858)
Walker, Josephine A. to James Maxey 10-29-1877
Walker, Kitty to Tillman Harris 1-6-1868 (6?-7-1868) B
Walker, Mahal to W. I. Pace 1-16-1860 (1-19-1860)
Walker, Marina to John Powers 7-15-1875 B
Walker, Martha to G. W. Maxey 12-22-1880 (12-29-1880)
Walker, Martha to W. H. Pace 12-9-1874 (12-10-1874)
Walker, Mary C. to Jas. C. Harris 2-1-1876 (2-3-1876)
Walker, Mary E. to L. L. Green 12-28-1865
Walker, Mary E. to Wm. C. Head 9-9-1869 (9-15-1869)
Walker, Mary E. to James D. Wall 12-18-1877
Walker, N. C. to B. Nicholson 5-10-1871 (5-11-1871)
Walker, Nannie E. to Wm. C. Hunt 4-15-1876 (4-27-1876)
Walker, R. A. to R. E. Justice 9-4-1875 (9-5-1875)
Walker, Sophrona to W. C. Hunter 9-16-1861 (9-17-1861)
Walker, Susan to James W. Walker 9-9-1868
Wall, Hannah to Scott Walker 7-27-1872 (7-27-1872) B

Wall, M. A. to L. F. Teasley 12-4-1866 (12-6-1866
Wall, Mary E. to Wilson Maxey 11-7-1874 (11-8-1874)
Walls, Sarah E. to L. D. Price 1-24-1866
Walls, Sarah F. to William Nanney 5-22-1878
Walton, Catie to Rufus Major 5-2-1872 (5-3-1872) B
Walton, George Ann to George W. Major 5-2-1872 (5-3-1872) B
Walton, Jennie to Lewis Teasley 6-9-1879 (6-13-1879) B
Warren, Lula (Miss) to J. B. Moorman 9-3-1878 (9-4-1878)
Washington, Hennie to Mark Williams 8-23-1879 B
Washington, Martha to Saml. Washington 12-16-1869 (12-26-1869) B
Washington, Nancy to Mack Merril 3-23-1871 B
Washington, Rachael to Marion Patterson 12-7-1878 (12-12-1878) B
Washington, Tempy to Andrew Dowlen 2-17-1868 (2-23-1868) B
Watkins, Elizabeth to Marshall Kerby 2-14-1868 B
Watson, Evaline to James Head 3-22-1871 B
Watson, Fillis Ann to Henry Walker 2-2-1878 (2-3-1878) B
Watson, Hannah to Buck Binkley 2-2-1870 (2-6-1870) B
Watson, Julia to Jordan Watson 12-24-1866 (12-27-1866) B
Watson, Margret to William Walkins 3-25-1869 B
Watson, Mattie to Benjamin Fikes 3-22-1871 B
Watt, Elizabeth to J. P. Bobett 10-1-1866 (10-3-1866)
Watt, Martha C. to G. W. Williams 11-20-1878 (no return)
Weakley, Car to J. W. Hogan 12-29-1856 (12-31-1856)
Weakley, Martha to J. D. Walker 2-5-1881 (2-13-1881)
Weakley, Martha M. to John L.? Eleazer 1-20-1868 (1-22-1868)
Weakley, Medora to J. W. Stack 8-12-1865
Weaklkey, P. to M. Page 12-24-1857
West, Sarah to Tobias Marlow 3-25-1874
Whelus, Mary C. to John J. Lee 12-10-1870 (12-11-1870)
White, Caroline to Edward Hogins 10-15-1868 B
White, Casanda to Calvin Brown 7-30-1874 (7-31-1875?) B
White, Eliza to George M. Forte? 8-3-1880 (8-4-1880) B
White, Mary to Joseph Knight 2-8-1878 (2-7?-1878) B
White, Sopia to Coral? Wilson 3-3-1880 (3-4-1880) B
Whitfield, Lucy C. to James D. Lewis 5-6-1876 (5-7-1876)
Whitfield, Susie A. to George J. Dillingham 12-29-1878
Whitfield, V. H. to W. C. Baker 12-24-1877 (12-25-1877)
Whitworth, Fredonia to G. D. Slack 3-8-1879 (3-13-1879)
Whitworth, Nancy A. to B. F. Shearon 8-4-1877 (8-9-1877)
Willi9ams, Jenney to Joshua Walker 5-18-1874 B
Williams, A. R. to John Hooper 4-29-1863
Williams, Allice C. to William D. Moses 1-7-1871 (1-8-1871)
Williams, Ann to Ben Dowlin 1-10-1879 B
Williams, Ann E. to George Alwell 6-21-1869 (7-1-1869)
Williams, Ann Mariah to Adam Walker 12-30-1873 B
Williams, Arena to Ben Dowlen 1-10-1879 B
Williams, C. H. to R. R. Felts 11-15-1878 (11-17-1878)
Williams, E. Bell to William Moore 1-26-1872 (1-13?-1872)
Williams, Edima? to Z. A. Woods 11-6-1880 (11-7-1880) B
Williams, Edna to Alex Barton 1-29-1880 B
Williams, F. E. to J. W. Harris 10-4-1880 (10-5-1880)
Williams, Harriet to Charter Teasley 1-27-1873 (1-30-1873) B
Williams, Jeraline to William Frazier 11-19-1877 (11-22-1877) B
Williams, Josephine to A. J. Denny 8-4-1869

Williams, Josie to A. J. Hunt 9-28-1876 (10-1-1876)
Williams, Judith to Johnson Davis 1-31-1880 B
Williams, Julia to Roger Pegram 10-26-1863 (10-28-1863)
Williams, Lucy to George T. Rowson 12-26-1868 (12-27-1868)
Williams, M. J. to Leonard Binkley 12-3-1864
Williams, Mamie to B. W. Waller 2-3-1872 (2-7-1872)
Williams, Marina to Levi Mallory 12-18-1879 (2-20-1879?) B
Williams, Martha A. C. to R. H. Inman 1-17-1868 (1-22-1868)
Williams, Martha K. to Hardridge Walker 1-18-1860 (1-19-1860)
Williams, Mary to James Everett 6-18-1874 B
Williams, Mexina to Levi Mallury 2-18-1879 (2-20-1879) B
Williams, Nancy A. to Thos. Bell 10-10-1871 (10-11-1871)
Williams, Nannie to A. M. Petway 7-24-1880
Williams, Rachel to R. T. Perry 9-26-1866
Williams, Rosell to Jack Mallory 12-26-1873 B
Williams, Rosetta to W. Teasly 2-8-1868 (2-22-1868) B
Williams, Unis to George Sherron 10-3-1870 (10-16-1870) B
Willis, Clora to Myatt Lee 1-20-1874 B
Willis, Edna to Granville Barton 3-17-1877 (3-18-1877) B
Willis, Florrence to James Craighead 4-14-1876 (4-16-1876) B
Willis, Susan T. to Wilson Willis 10-24-1870 (10-25-1870)
Willson, Calvina T. to John R.? Stack 2-25-1868 (2-27-1868)
Wilson, Eliza to Henry Dowlen 8-31-1874 B
Wilson, Elizabeth to Moses Dye 1-18-1866 (6?-18-1866) B
Wilson, Mahala to Woody Page 2-7-1880 (2-10-1880)
Wilson, Milla Jane to Anderson Sayer 11-16-1867 (12-4-1867) B
Wilson, Nancy to David Dowlen 1-28-1874 (1-29-1874) B
Wilson, Nancy Jane to Franklin Adcock 8-25-1866 (8-30-1866)
Wilson, Olive W. S. to Willie W. Hunt 3-11-1868 (3-12-1868)
Wilson, Rebeca to A. Knight 12-2-1867 (12-12-1867)
Wilson, Sarah to J. D. Vanhook 8-3-1857
Wilson, Susan A. to Z. T. Walker 4-21-1875 (4-22-1875)
Woodall, E. J. to A. E. Snell 4-14-1862
Woodall, L. A. to E. T. Wren 12-21-1858 (12-23-1858)
Woodall, Martha to J. T. Walker 4-11-1878 (4-14-1878)
Woodmore, Louisa to Willy Bell 9-27-1876 (9-28-1876) B
Woodson, Ivone H. to W. W. Scott 5-28-18878 (5-29-1878)
Woodson, Mary to Andrew Dowlen 7-4-1866 (7-8-1866) B
Woodson, Nancy to Thomas Garrett 2-12-1869 (2-13-1869) B
Woodward, A. T. to J. B. Bartee 12-6-1859 (12-13-1859)
Woodward, Charlotte to Lewis Drake 12-24-1871 (1-21-1872) B
Woodward, F. Y. P. to Geo. W. Ramer 6-1-1857 (6-11-1857)
Woodward, Harriet to John B. Hall 9-14-1873 (9-23-1873)
Woodward, S. O. to S. G. Eleazier 5-1-1858 (5-5-1858)
Work, E. C. to W. L. Cullum 3-2-1868 (3-3-1868)
Work, Elizabeth to E. G. Cullum 3-2-1868
Work, Launa J. to J. M. Eatherly 10-21-1871 (10-25-1871)
Work, V. C. to J. W. Adams 9-25-1880 (9-26-1880)
Works, Alice to Ander Shooks 7-21-1881 B
Wright, S. A. W. to R. A. Reeves 9-11-1876 (9-14-1876)
Wyatt, Martha to Andrew Travis 9-13-1873 (9-17-1873)
Wynn, Lueaser to William W. Deal 9-23-1872 (9-24-1872)
Wynn, M. E. to Robt. T. Scott 10-6-1869 (10-7-1869)
Wynn, Mary E. to W. H. Scott 9-24-1866 (9-25-1866)

Yeatman, Tama to James Redding 8-25-1877 (8-26-1877) B
York, Harriet to C. F. Williams 10-28-1874
Young, Samuel Eller to Stephen Donil? 6-25-1867 (7-4-1867)